Paddling
the
Pacific Northwest

Copyright © 2013 Wayne J. Lutz

All rights reserved. No part of this publication may be reproduced, stored in a retrieval system, or transmitted, in any form or by any means, electronic, mechanical, photocopying, recording, or otherwise, without the written prior permission of the author. Reviewers are authorized to quote short passages within a book review, as permitted under the United States Copyright Act of 1976.

Note for Librarians: a catalog record for this book that includes Dewey Decimal Classification and U.S. Library of Congress numbers is available from the Library and Archives of Canada. The complete catalog record can be obtained from their online database at:
www.collectionscanada.ca/amicus/index-e.html

ISBN 9781927438152
Printed in the United States of America

Powell River Books
Powell RIver, BC
Book sales online at:
www.powellriverbooks.com
phone: 604-483-1704
email: wlutz@mtsac.edu

10 9 8 7 6 5 4 3 2 1

Paddling
the
Pacific Northwest

Wayne J. Lutz

2013
Powell River Books

To Margy, my paddling companion
in water both slow and swift

*The stories are true, and the characters are real.
Some details are adjusted to protect the guilty.
All of the mistakes rest solidly with the author.*

The author is a recreational kayaker who attempts to provide information regarding recommended paddling procedures. However, much of the material contained in this book involves personal techniques, navigational data that may be outdated, and individual recommendations that could prove hazardous to the operation of a canoe or kayak. The author and publisher take no responsibility for the accuracy of any of the methods or materials described in this book.

Front Cover Photo:
Sea kayak at Rasar State Park, Birdsview WA

Books by Wayne J. Lutz

Costal British Columbia Stories
Up the Lake
Up the Main
Up the Winter Trail
Up the Strait
Up the Airway
Farther Up the Lake
Farther Up the Main
Farther Up the Strait
Cabin Number 5
Off the Grid
Up the Inlet

Science Fiction Titles
Echo of a Distant Planet
Inbound to Earth
Anomaly at Fortune Lake
When Galaxies Collide
Across the Galactic Sea

Paccific Northwest Series
FLying the Pacific Northwest
Paddling the Pacific Northwest

www.PowellRiverBooks.com

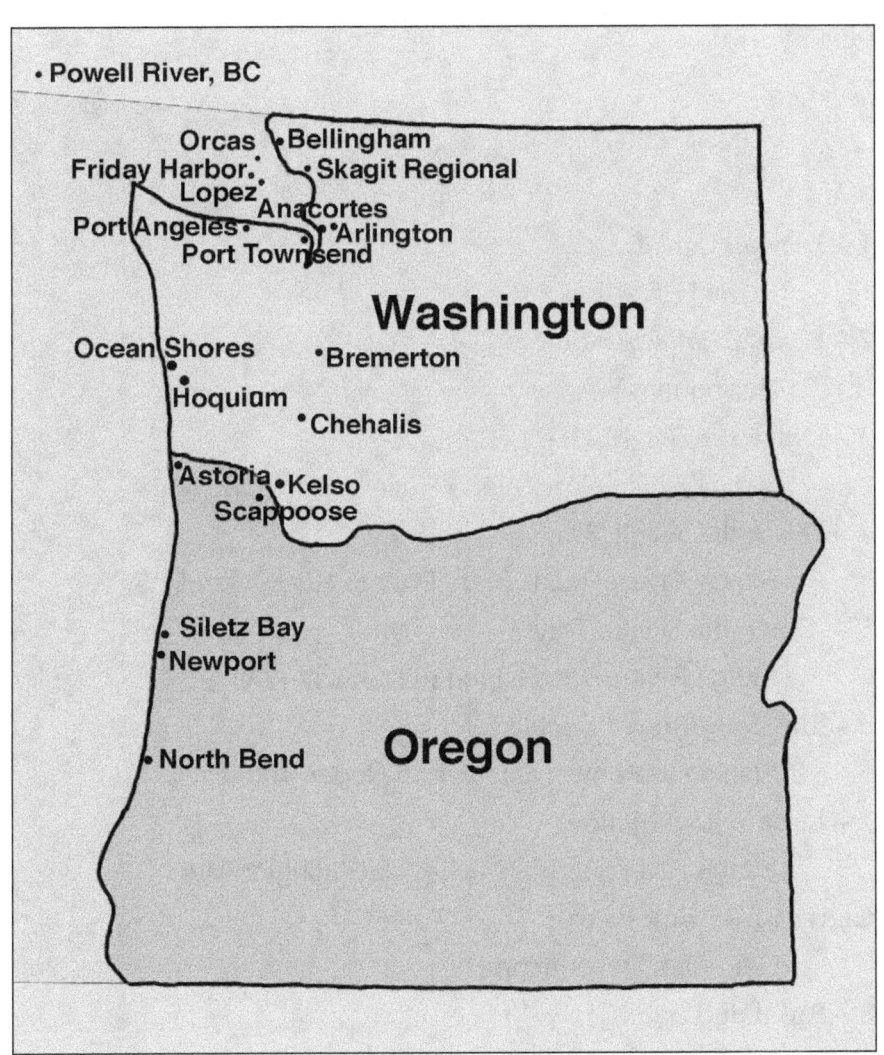

Washington and Oregon destinations featured in this book

Contents

1 – Leaving Canada 10
    Powell River BC

2 – River Trip Preparation 20
    Bellingham WA

3 – Down the Skagit: Day 1 25
    Skagit River: Concrete to Rasar State Park WA

4 – Down the Skagit: Day 2 40
    Skagit River: Rasar State Park to Ross Island WA

5 – Down the Skagit: Day 3 58
    Skagit River: Ross Island to Conway WA

6 – The Complicated Simple Life 68
    Fishing the Lower Skagit and Upper Nooksack

7 – Little Yellow Mango 77
    Skagit River: Sedro-Woolley to Burlington WA

CENTER-OF-BOOK PHOTOS 87
    Canadian Destinations

8 – Paddling Lesson 92
    South Fork of Nooksack River WA

9 – Water, Water, Everywhere · · · · · · · · · 102
    Skagit River: Hamilton to Lyman WA

10 – No Shuttle Required · · · · · · · · · · · 109
    Silver Lake WA

11 – Saltwater or Fresh? · · · · · · · · · · · 115
    Dakota Creek WA

12 – City Lakes · · · · · · · · · · · · · · · 125
    Lake Samish, Bellingham WA

13 – Up the Creek · · · · · · · · · · · · · · 131
    California Creek WA

14 – Williamette River · · · · · · · · · · · · 138
    Corvallis to Albany OR

15 – Go North, Young Man · · · · · · · · · · 153
    Fraser River BC

About the Author · · · · · · · · · · · · · · · 172

Geographic Index · · · · · · · · · · · · · · · 174

Chapter 1

Leaving Canada
Powell River BC

It's hard to imagine a better home for a sea kayak than the south coast of British Columbia, particularly since I live there. So why would a two-person Current Designs Libra XT move across the border to my part-time home in the United States, with all of BC still to explore? The answer lies in the difference between rivers in British Columbia and those in Washington and Oregon.

Rivers for a sea kayak? Yes, rivers, especially those of a very special kind – what I call "gentle pushers." These meandering giants flow constantly downhill, but never with the vengeance of rapids and waterfalls. Try to find these in British Columbia. (Oh, wait, there's the nearby Fraser River, but I don't think of that obvious choice until much later.)

In it's early years, my Libra XT was both a sea and lake vessel that explored the gunkholes of BC's south coast and Vancouver Island, moving occasionally onto lakes, with an extended stay at my floating cabin on Powell Lake. *Mr. Kayak* was an ideal fit for this mix of fresh and salt water.

Overnight adventures in my sea kayak included the Copeland Islands of Desolation Sound, the Gulf Islands, and coastal lakes named Lois, Khartoum, Nanton, Powell, and Horseshoe. *Mr. Kayak's* Canadian life is documented in several books in the series subtitled *Coastal British Columbia Stories*, including *Up the Lake*, *Up the Strait*, and *Off the Grid*.

When not in the water, the sea kayak sat atop my 1989 Ford Tempo, a car originally purchased as an airport clunker that later became the dry land foundation on which my kayak slept during extended periods

Libra XT at Lang Bay, British Columbia

of hibernation. For many months (especially off-season), *Mr. Kayak* resided at my float cabin on Powell Lake, where I enjoyed tranquil hours on the never-freezing (too deep) lake, drift fishing and paddling short distances.

Kayak aimed at float cabin site, Hole in Wall, Powell Lake, BC

Before leaving Canada, the kayak's latter years were spent in an open-ended hangar at Powell River Airport, awaiting the call for another ocean or lake adventure. *Mr. Kayak* had never seen a river of any size, nor had I imagined paddling this vessel in any location other than Canada. Then I read a book about kayaking in the Arctic.

I'm influenced heavily by what I read. One moment, based on a science fiction tale, I'll imagine myself rocketing to the Andromeda Galaxy. Then I'll find myself preparing to scale Mount Everest. Now, while reading about a canoe trip across northern Canada, I'm ready for a big river.

During my armchair adventures in the Canadian Arctic and the Barrens, reading *Water and Sky: Reflections of a Northern Year*, I follow Alan Kesselheim as he describes his 14-month canoe odyssey, 2000 miles across Canada. I hang on every word.

The chapters that particularly intrigue me are those where the author glides down miles of "gentle pushers," the great rivers of the north that require no paddling, except an occasional steering blade dipped into the water. But usually it's followed by an upstream struggle on a river rising into the mountains, or a wind-caused battle on a lake, reminding me of my personal crusades on Canada's lakes and along ocean shores. What I'm looking for are meandering rivers where I can drift downhill for days, being pushed in a persistent but gentle manner. Call it constructive laziness – a desire to harness the power of gravity, without risking a dangerous plunge.

British Columbia, of course, has plenty of rivers that meet the downhill criteria, but you won't find any in southern BC navigable by amateurs (until I eventually discover the nearby Fraser). Plunging drops and cascading waterfalls don't suit *Mr. Kayak*. My trusty sea kayak isn't the kind of vessel designed for overly exciting rivers. And neither is Margy.

Margy is my wife, Margaret, my partner in most of my voyages by kayak. She loves the same on-water adventures and camping experiences that enthrall me, with the exception of strong currents. On one of our first kayak trips, I led her through Dodd Narrows (near Nanaimo, BC), when the tidal current was running fast. I remember yelling out joyously as we darted through the whitewater and whirlpools. And I remember her screaming out in an entirely different manner. Maybe it was just a bad first encounter, but it produced a lasting memory for

Margy of the most negative kind. Whitewater is simply not her thing, and I must accept it if I'm to enjoy her company on any river adventure. Thus, I seek the elusive meandering downhill push, without the added punctuation of strong currents and raging whitewater. Which leads me across the border to the State of Washington.

* * * * *

DRIVING DOWN INTERSTATE-5 TOWARDS SEATTLE from my part-time American home in Bellingham brings me across bridges spanning mighty rivers that pour into the Pacific. The biggest of them all is the Skagit River, which dumps more freshwater into Puget Sound than all of Washington's other rivers combined. The view from my car crossing the Interstate-5 bridge near Burlington (site of a major structural collapse in 2013) provides majestic panoramas up and down the Skagit, where it meanders in a wide swath as it approaches the ocean delta. Of course, this wide river winds more violently farther upstream, but the lower reaches are exactly the kind of gentle pusher I'm seeking.

As an alternate to the Skagit, I briefly survey the Nooksack River, as I cross it heading south to Bellingham from the border crossing at the Peace Arch. From this bridge (also on I-5), the river view in both directions is enticing – narrower than the Skagit, but flowing steadily towards the sea. I can envision myself navigating down the Nooksack with a contented Margy in the front cockpit.

Thus begins my active searching for my first gentle pusher, and an immediate realization that my dream isn't far-fetched. There are many rivers near Bellingham meeting the criteria of slow and meandering. To get things started, it's only a matter of moving *Mr. Kayak* from Canada to Bellingham.

* * * * *

MY FORD TEMPO IS A TRUSTY OLD VEHICLE, with emphasis on the word "old" (1989). Until now, the mileage has been limited to British Columbia roads near my home on Powell Lake, including excursions with the kayak on top. The big yellow banana looks even bigger on top of a small compact car, but the Tempo handles highway speeds up to 60 miles per hour before the stabilizing tie-down ropes begins to sing, an indication *Mr. Kayak* is trying to go airborne, and it's time to slow down.

Mr. Kayak on Tempo at Shinglemill, Powell Lake, BC

If the Ford is to come south with the kayak, some work will be needed before attempting any remote adventures. The driver's window is jammed in the closed or (with a push) open position, and the muffler is emitting way too much noise on the highway to satisfy local law enforcement. These inconveniences can await our arrival in the States, where a visit to the repair shop should include a good overall safety check before we launch on any distant kayaking adventures. I add a cylinder compression check to the list of pending inspections, as well as an overall test drive by an expert to assure the transmission isn't on its last legs. Going up a sizable hill at highway speed has become increasingly traumatic for this gutless wonder, and I'm not sure how much of it might be due to the obviously damaged muffler or tailpipe, low compression, or faulty transmission. In any case, we'll deal with these issues as soon as we get to Bellingham. If we get to States, that is.

Before loading the kayak at the airport hangar in town where *Mr. Kayak* has been stored, I use gelcoat cleaner to spiff up the hull and top deck. The yellow Libra has faded from years of exposure to afternoon sun in the open-ended hangar and seasonal bouts of blowing dirt. The open cockpits are coated with a layer of grime. But after a few hours of manual labor, *Mr. Kayak* looks almost like new, and lot happier.

I use buckets of water from the Westview Flying Club to leak test the interior holds, including the cockpit, noting where water leaks from one bulkhead to the next. The results are not surprising – everything seems adequately sealed except for the center cargo hold, which has experienced minor leaks in the past. I use a sponge and rag to dry out the holds, and then apply silicon waterproof sealant to the bulkhead walls between the forward cockpit and the center hatch. I even add a thin bead of sealant along all bulkheads I can reach.

Bob, my hangar neighbor, is working next door on the landing gear of his fabric-covered airplane. So when my spiff-up is complete, I ask him to help me hoist the kayak onto the Tempo.

"We're going to put that thing up there?" he asks. "How long is it?"

"Twenty feet, one of the biggest sea kayaks they sell."

"And one of the smallest cars," he adds.

The two of us easily manage the empty kayak today, but it's always on the borderline when Margy and I need to lift it. Margy is strong, but short. We've hoisted *Mr. Kayak* on and off the Tempo many times, but it's necessary to park on a level surface or where the bow is headed slightly downslope. It's important to position the Tempo carefully when only Margy and I are available for lifting, which is most of the time. The stern of the vessel is considerably heavier than the front, so that's my end. Margy's end of the kayak is right at her hoisting limit, both in terms of height and weight, and my end nearly maxes me out.

As much as we laugh about the old Tempo, it's the perfect carrier for *Mr. Kayak*. Standard Canadian Tire rooftop racks won't attach to most modern cars because of their molded window design. Additionally, our Ford's low roof height yields a shorter lift. When Margy and I are raising the empty kayak, even a few inches of advantage is appreciated.

Bob and I handle the lift without complications. Now, with the big yellow banana in its road-travel position, I secure it with straps and ropes, then go through a checklist I've developed for overnight kayak equipment that fills the trunk – paddles, sleeping bags, tent, air mattresses, ground cloth, spray skirts, water hand pump, life vests, aqua-slippers, kayak caddy wheels (the most-bulky item), folding chairs, waterproof containers.

My preparation for the trip to the States is drawing to a close. The trunk is nearly full, *Mr. Kayak* is secure on top of the Tempo, and the car is reasonably ready to travel. For now, I pull as far into the hangar as possible to get the best protection from the weather. It'll be another week before we're ready to head south.

* * * * *

MR. KAYAK ATOP THE TEMPO is a bit of a curiosity at the ferry terminal. The mix of vehicles is always unusual on these ferry routes, but the contrast between the size of the kayak and the diminutive stature of the car turns a few heads.

"No, it's a kayak, Tommy," says a mother to her inquisitive son. "Looks like they're going on a big trip."

Yes, this is a big trip for the Tempo – all the way to the United States. The muffler is getting louder all the time, so I make sure I'm one of the last vehicles to engage the starter in the ferry line.

Two ferries later, we arrive at Horseshoe Bay (Vancouver), where Margy will drive the final leg to the border-crossing at Aldergrove. We face two remaining problems – the loud muffler when we pull up to the border kiosk and the fickle driver's window. Today, this electric window is jammed closed.

"I'll just stop and open the door to talk to the border agent," says Margy, but I know this makes her uncomfortable.

"Might not make them happy," I reply. "We don't need to aggravate them, under the circumstances."

"Circumstances?" she says. "You mean the kayak."

"The big yellow banana, and the BC plates to accompany our U.S. passports. To say nothing of the muffler."

It's all perfectly legal, of course (except for the muffler), but it's bound to set off some what's-going-on alarms at the kiosk. U.S. passports, car occupants claiming their permanent residency is in Canada (thus, making the Canadian plates legal), and what about this big kayak headed for the States? You can't bring any vehicle or vessel across the border without officially importing it, unless you're taking it back to Canada after a visit. Are we stealing this unregistered boat from Canada, planning to sell it in the States? Then, of course, there's the muffler and the window that can't be rolled down. Add it all up, and we've undoubtedly got some questions to answer. I can hear our expected greeting: "Just pull forward and park over there. Then go inside and give them this piece of paper." Been there, done that – not a pleasant experience.

"Pull over at the next turnout," I tell Margy. "I'll try to get the window down."

It works! With Margy operating the electric window button, I push inward and down on the glass. There's a terrible grinding sound, but the window jerks downward, and now it's fully open. We enter the border lineup as an almost-normal arrival, except for a huge kayak on a tiny old car with Canadian plates, U.S. passports, and a roaring muffler.

"Hello! Where do you live?" asks the smiling border agent, as Margy hands our passports to him through the fully-open car window.

"We live in Powell River, British Columbia," answers Margy, as the agent swipes our passports and glances at his computer screen.

Powell Lake, where we live, is adjacent to Powell River, the official municipality. So that's the best answer.

"Anything to declare?" he asks.

"Nothing today," says Margy nonchalantly.

"Have a good day," he replies.

Welcome to America.

* * * * *

OUR FRIEND, JEANNE, who lives in our condo complex in Bellingham, is waiting for us. She's seen the Tempo and the kayak in Canada, but never together, one atop the other. Her condo unit overlooks the outside parking area, and she hears us coming.

"I knew you'd be pulling in soon, so I was in the kitchen keeping an eye out, when I heard you pulling into the lot. That engine is really loud."

"Needs a new muffler or tailpipe," I reply.

"I watched you try to fit into the parking spot. Rather tight."

"It's a compact car. But the kayak sticks out a ways."

The plan is to store the yellow banana under the wing of our Piper Arrow, in the hangar at Bellingham Airport. (Did I mention we're airport people? – big time! If it weren't for airport hangars, we'd never be able to store all our recreational equipment.) But it's getting late, and I'm tired from the all-day trip. It's only 100 miles between Powell

River and Bellingham, but it takes eight hours, with two ferries and lots of winding road. Do the math, and it's an average speed of 12 miles per hour, a rather long day. So we'd like to leave the kayak at the condo overnight. Yet it's a tempting target for hell-raising kids, so I should move it into the underground garage.

I reposition the Tempo in front of the garage gate, get out of the car, and eyeball the situation. Using a tape measure, I determine the highest point on the kayak, then walk into the garage and measure the overhead lights I'll be driving under. Technically, this should work, but the clearance is only a few inches, making for an adrenaline-producing slow drive through the garage. Margy walks beside the Tempo, with a continual forward wave from her arm and constant reassurances of "It's okay!"

Once in the underground parking spot assigned to my condo unit, the kayak sticks out too far from the yellow-lined limits. But the parking space next to mine is Jeanne's, where her small car can be edged to the side. So with a lot of maneuvering, I secure the car-topped kayak at an odd angle, barely within the marked borders.

In the garage at Bellingham, WA

Early the next morning, I'm awakened by a telephone call.

"Mr. Lutz, a resident has reported a big car with a kayak on top that's parked in your stall," says the condo management representative. "And it's sticking out into the driving lane."

I'm, of course, not happy, but neither am I surprised. Besides, I successfully avoided a trip to the airport yesterday when I was tired.

"Tell the whiner I'm moving it right now," I say in a purposeful angry tone, which is all for show.

It isn't clear whether the representatives "Okay" reply is serious or not. But I laugh when I hang up, so she doesn't misinterpret my often-misinterpreted sense of humor. Hopefully, she knows I'm not really angry.

At the airport hangar, with the help of Margy and Jeanne, we unload the kayak, and tuck it under the wing of the Piper Arrow. *Mr. Kayak* is in a convenient storage location, on it's dolly, with the caddy wheels positioned near the stern. Our Piper Arrow still can be pulled in and out of the hangar without needing to move the kayak. Walking around the airplane inside the hangar is awkward, but a big step over the kayak's hull is certainly acceptable. This is a comfortable new home for the big yellow banana in a fully enclosed hangar, quite a luxury for a kayak accustomed to spending 10 years on top of a car, moored in Powell Lake, or exposed to the weather in an open-ended hangar. Still, I wonder if *Mr. Kayak* is lonely during those dark nights indoors. Hopefully, the Arrow and the kayak strike a companionable international friendship.

Chapter 2

River Trip Preparation
Bellingham WA

THE SKAGIT RIVER WILL BE FIRST. It's the biggest and most obvious gentle pusher. And it's a short distance south on Interstate-5.

For advance reconnaissance, I look over river charts and review several books regarding paddling the rivers of the Pacific Northwest. My personal favorites are *Paddling Washington* (The Mountaineers Books) and *Sea Kayaking from Mountains to Ocean* by Dan Baharav. *Paddling Washington* concentrates on data for whitewater passages, but makes a good overall guide with excellent overview charts. Dan Baharav's book is more of an essay description of the journeys (without charts), but provides the flavor of the routes.

Margy and I have a special advantage in route planning – our Piper Arrow. On a flight back to Bellingham from Oregon, we divert up the Skagit River to look over the lower reaches from ground elevations of 2500 hundred feet in the east to sea level at the delta. One picture is worth a thousand words.

Our aerial reconnaissance confirms what I've read in the guidebooks – the Skagit flows through populated areas below the town of Concrete, but you won't see much of humanity from the bed of the river. From aboard the Arrow, it appears to be an easy route all the way to the delta. Then again, everything looks close together in an aerial view. Often I find it disappointing to see a region from the Arrow that I want to explore on the ground, either by powerboat or kayak. It all looks too easy from the Arrow, and a lot more challenging from the water. There are places I've looked down on in British Columbia that appear to be a simple hop from Powell Lake. In fact, they're destinations requiring several days of travel by boat.

Aerial view looking up the Skagit River near Burlington, WA

Out the window of the airplane, I snap another photo of the lower reaches of the river I'd like to explore below Interstate-5. Near Mount Vernon, the Skagit meanders around a huge bend that has nearly become a cutoff oxbow lake. In this part of the river, it travels right

Aerial view of lower Skagit River at Mount Vernon, WA

through town, including past a wide gravel beach and the downtown area. I don't paddle a kayak so I can visit cities, but this appears to be a unique chance to cut right through a busy metropolis. And it's appropriate to remember that this will be a good place to indulge in a restaurant meal.

* * * * *

BEFORE WE CAN BEGIN OUR FIRST RIVER TRIP IN THE STATES, the Tempo needs repairs. The window and muffler are obvious, but the compression check and transmission evaluation are scarier from a cost standpoint, although I still need to know their condition. Surprisingly, the compression and transmission are in good shape: "They don't make them like this any more," says the mechanic.

However, the window repair will be delayed until a motor can be found in a junkyard. And just as the repair shop is about to roll the old Ford out of the shop, they find a leaking fuel tank, which has to be replaced. Win some, lose some.

One of the biggest joys in any project is the planning phase. As a pilot, I'm used to checklists, and I develop a detailed one for our first river adventure. After the first trip, I should be able to tweak the list even further, eventually coming up with a quick pack-and-go procedure.

If you plan to travel in a kayak, particularly if you're staying overnight, a personal checklist is essential. What you put on your list is very much a personal thing, but here are some of the essentials I recommend:

Water (bottle in each cockpit, plus large stored jugs)
Insect repellent
Suntan lotion
Cell phone (in waterproof bag or case)
Cash plus credit card (leave your wallet locked in the car)
GPS (even city road charts show good river outlines)
Camera (in waterproof bag or case)
Spare batteries for GPS and camera
Kayak guidebook
Paper map (sealed in plastic bag)
Sunglasses
Safari hat (or hat with sun protection for face, ears and neck)
Water slippers or boots
Extra socks (never too many dry socks)
Prescription medicines, and some headache pills

Pocket notebook and pen (to update your checklist)
Gloves (fingerless preferred, except in winter)
Band-aids
Neosporin or other anti-bacterial ointment
Toilet paper
Swiss army knife (or your preferred knife tool)
Jacket or sweatshirt (regardless of temperature)
Shoes for hiking
Snack bars, trail mix, and small boxed juices
Towel

Overnight added items:
Tent, sleeping bag, air mattress, ground cover tarp
Book and reading light (reading glasses, if needed)
Flashlight with spare batteries
Portable radio
Toothbrush and toothpaste
Daily vitamins
Mini-meals (unless carrying cooking equipment)
    Sealed fruit cups (no refrigeration needed)
    Crackers with peanut butter or cheese (prepackaged)
    More snack bars
    More juice packs or pouches (no refrigeration required)
    Sealed pudding cups (no refrigeration required)
    Spoons
Garbage bags (also good for waterproofing stored items)
Extra plastic sealable bags (never too many)
Tide tables (if applicable)

* * * * *

YOU'LL NOTICE THAT NOTHING on the above list requires refrigeration. But cool is good, and I'd recommend a small ice chest, the soft type that can be stuffed into a cargo hold. For ice, we freeze several small water bottles, filled nearly to the top, and keep them in the freezer until the morning of departure. These ice bottles serve for cooling in the small ice chest, and we drink the water as it melts. In fact, on our first Skagit River trip during the heat of August, we sacrificed the recently melted water as a down-the-river treat right away, using it as the first water bottles in our cockpits. By the next morning, at our campsite, only a small amount of ice remained, but the ice-cold water sure hit the spot during travel on the river! I still remember the wonderful taste of cold water trickling down my throat at our first stop at Rasar State Park.

Sodas are a luxury on a river trip, but keeping them cold only works until the ice is gone on the second day. So bring a few, and enjoy them on the first day out.

Think "space" regarding everything on your personal checklist. For us, our checklist allows us to pack adequately for several nights on the river with a partially-empty center cargo hold. The Libra XT is so large that the center compartment is advertised as a third cockpit for a child or dog. Our forward and aft compartments provide enough room for most of our gear, along with a few essential on-river items carried in the forward and aft cockpits. However, Margy and I are content to go several days without cooked meals. We usually plan our river stops at small towns to enjoy an afternoon restaurant-cooked meal that serves as our evening meal, followed by a snack later at the campsite. For breakfast and lunch, snacks serve us just fine. You could bring boxed (non-refrigerated) milk containers, if you prefer cereal. The big problem with full meals is the extra equipment you need to pack for cooking (Coleman stove, dishes, and utensils). Make up your mind regarding your personal level of tolerance and food comfort, and adjust accordingly.

* * * * *

SO NOW WE'RE PREPARED, with a pile of items from the checklist sitting in the den, the kayak in the hangar, the Tempo in the condo parking lot, and Jeanne ready to assist. Her help is a big luxury, because now we have the missing link – transportation to the launch site and a ride back home at the end of our first trip on the Skagit. Shuttling vehicles is an alternative, but there's nothing like having a friend who can serve your drop-off and pickup needs.

All three of us are ready to go. We'll leave leisurely at noon tomorrow, giving us a chance to get our bearings on our first day out without making the first leg of our three-day river trip an arduous journey.

Chapter 3

Down the Skagit: Day 1
Skagit River: Concrete to Rasar State Park WA

WE DRIVE TO THE AIRPORT AT NOON, with Jeanne at the wheel of the Tempo. She reaches out the sometimes-functioning driver's window (parts still on order) to place my airport gate card against the electronic reader. The gray box on the post beeps normally, but nothing happens. The gate remains closed, and we're on the outside of the airport fence looking in. Jeanne tries again, another normal beep, and nothing happens (again).

"Let me see the card," I say.

When she hands it to me, I look it over closely, and finally see the problem. The expiration date is two days overdue. It's a Sunday, so there's no way to renew the card today. We obviously need some help just to get to our kayak.

A young fellow in the parking lot behind us is just getting onto his motorcycle. What he's doing here isn't clear, but he's the only person in sight, so it's worth a try.

"Hi!" I say, as I approach his now-running motorcycle.

I raise my voice so he can hear me through his helmet and over the sound of his motor. I hand him my gate card.

"Can you help us?" I ask. "This card just expired, and we really need to get through the gate."

Normally, I wouldn't think of asking for assistance like this. Airport officials take gate security seriously, and they should. And I always adhere to the letter of the law around airport property. But now it's a weekend, with the airport office closed. And I'm stuck in the middle, with an airport ID expired by two days. Margy has a gate card, too, but hers is back in the condo. So we're valid customers (sort of), but without a ticket to get in.

The young fellow gives me a suspicious look, as he should. Then he removes his helmet, motorcycle engine still running, and looks closely at my card.

"It's two days out of date," he replies. "Won't find anybody to talk to on a Sunday."

"Right," I reply, hoping he's thinking this through.

Obviously, the motorcyclist could get in trouble helping us through the gate, even in these circumstances. I give him time to ponder his decision without further interference.

"Okay," he says, shutting down his motorcycle, stepping off, and setting his helmet on the seat.

He pulls out a plastic card and walks over to the Tempo, where Jeanne is still poised at the gate, Margy is in the back seat, and my passenger door is still open. "Beep," and the gate opens. We're in!

At the hangar, we open the big doors, and roll the yellow banana out into the August noontime sun. Once the kayak is positioned alongside the Tempo, Margy prepares the roof rack pads, while Jeanne and I watch.

At the hangar in Bellingham

"Anything I can do," asks Jeanne.

"Not really," I reply. "It's pretty much a two-person job, but you can help balance the kayak on Margy's end when we lift it onto the roof."

"Oh, my!" is her reply.

Jeanne is pleased to help out today, but she isn't sure she fully understands how we're going to get this big kayak on top of this car, to say nothing of how we're going to traverse the route down the river. But she's a good sport, ready to drive us to our launch point with a smile.

We lift the kayak with no difficulties, and secure it on the Tempo's roof rack. I walk back to the gate entrance to try to find someone who will let us out. Near the gate, a hangar door is open, so I walk in, with my expired card in hand.

"Maybe you'd be willing to help some poor Canadians," I say. "My gate card has expired, and we need to get our kayak out."

"Sure, sure," says a gray-haired fellow with a thick beard. "Canucks trying to steal another kayak from our airport, eh?"

"No, no. Honest, it's mine, but my gate card expired two days ago."

The bearded man steps outside the hangar with me, just as Jeanne and Margy drive up.

"Mighty big kayak," says the man.

"It just looks big," I reply. "Tiny car."

"Homeland Security would love to get hold of you," says the man.

He clicks his gate card against the electronic reader, which beeps and sends a get-outta-here signal to the gate. We're gone!

* * * * *

JEANNE DRIVES, WHILE I RIDE in the front passenger seat, Margy in back. The Tempo's driver's window is jammed half-closed, although it worked briefly at the airport, and now the temperamental car transfers its electrical illness to the other windows. My passenger window and the right rear window are stuck in the closed position. The left rear window opens halfway, which is normal for this older design. Which makes for a mighty uncomfortable drive in the August sun. I turn up the recirculation fan to max, but we can forget the air conditioner – it died years ago.

With some adept hand movement, Jeanne angles her hand out her partially-open window to blow some air my way. We hurtle down Interstate-5 as fast as we can to keep the air moving. I advise Jeanne to set her speed below 60, but the stabilizing ropes begin to sing at 50, so she has to slow down.

"Maybe your slightly-open window make the ropes seem noisier today," I announce.

"Feels like something bad is about to happen," replies Jeanne. "Is the kayak supposed to be shifting around like that?"

"It's all pretty normal," I report. "You'll get lots of warning if *Mr. Kayak* is about to depart the roof."

She gives me a look that could kill.

Just then, as if on cue, a cop car passes on our left, accelerates briefly in front of us, and maneuvers into the right lane again to take the next exit ramp.

"Must be afraid to drive behind us," I suggest.

"I don't blame him," replies Jeanne.

* * * * *

WE EXIT I-5 AT ROUTE 20, which will take us along the Skagit River all the way to Concrete, about 30 miles. The river distance, due to its pronounced meandering is at least twice as far.

At Sedro-Woolley, we drive down to the Skagit River at the waterfront RV park, a location Margy and I visited last month. Standing on the paved boat ramp, we look out over the river, trying to judge how fast the water is running compared to earlier in the summer.

"Not quite as fast, don't you think?" I ask.

"Looks mighty swift to me," replies Margy. "If we try to bring the kayak to shore here and miss the ramp, we'll never be able to paddle back upstream."

There's a look in her eye that bothers me. She views the river with suspicion, as if she feels she's in over her head. From my viewpoint, all looks fine, and I'm glad we're going to get a good push from the river.

"It won't be a problem. We're not planning to stop here anyway. But I'm sure we could paddle upstream against this current. In fact, I think a single paddler could do it – easy."

Sedro-Wooley launch ramp

"Not easy," is her simple reply.

This has bothered her ever since we first stood on this ramp in July and surveyed the flowing water. When we reviewed the kayak guidebooks, she kept reminding me this river flows fast, and can be dangerous during floods (which isn't during the summer). And there are logjams everywhere, according to the guides, although I interpret these conditions to be minor and easily navigated. She considers the situation otherwise.

"Once we're underway, you'll see how gentle things are," I state. "There isn't any whitewater to worry about," I add. "Just a gentle push all the way down the river. Exactly what we've been looking for."

"We or you?" she asks confrontationally.

She's right. I've been the one seeking such a river. Now I've found it, and Margy is balking. I want her to feel comfortable, and I'm sure she'll be fine as soon as we get going. Sometimes the best medicine is to simply get started.

* * * * *

Our next stop is Rasar State Park near Birdsview, where we plan to spend our first night. I plan to mark a GPS waypoint at a prospective spot where we'll bring the kayak to shore. There's no launch ramp here, but I expect to find considerable beach area that should be adequate. And I've already made a campsite reservation; just to be sure our first night out is controlled and comfortable. The second night will, hopefully, be on a remote island in the river, but tonight will be restrained and relaxed. We need a good start to our trip to assure we feel comfortable about what lies ahead.

Since I knew we'd be stopping here, I've come up with an efficient plan that might be a bit of overkill. Since we're stopping here to evaluate the nearby river landing, why not drop our camping equipment off at our assigned site. Of course, we could continue to Concrete, load our camping gear in the kayak there, paddle downstream to the state park, and then unload and bag-drag to our campsite. That's a lot of extra effort, since we're already here now. So we find our assigned site, and pile our tent, sleeping bags, and air mattresses on the picnic table. This will result in an easy walk from the beach when we arrive by kayak. The only bag-drag will be one-way downhill to the beach in the morning.

It's a brilliant plan, unless, of course, we run into problems in the short first segment of our downstream paddle. What if it takes longer than we expect, and we arrive late? Wouldn't it be better to simply stop on a riverbank and pitch our tent there, especially if it's getting dark? Yes, but that won't work if we don't have our camping gear in the kayak. Or what if Margy is right? – Suppose we're being pushed too fast to pull onto the beach properly, go sailing right on by, and can't generate the energy required to paddle back to the park. That's the tradeoff, and I'm willing to take it. Margy doesn't question my wisdom, which is a good sign she's feeling more comfortable about the river now. It's a beautiful state park, and we look forward to spending the night here.

We walk to the beach, which is a dirt trail that leads to several informal swimming spots where a few families are gathered on the shore and (briefly) in the cold water. I mark a GPS waypoint at the spot we agree looks best for coming ashore. Easy!

I glance at the sun, still high in the afternoon sky, but time is slipping away quickly. We had a late start, with several stops along the way. Rather than set up our tent now, I suggest we leave it until we return with the kayak.

"Let's get going now," I say. "Maybe we can find a place to eat that will be take care of our early evening meal. Then we can launch the kayak near the bridge that crosses the river at Concrete."

I'm thinking "fast food" here, more because of the escaping time than lack of appetite. The worst thing that could happen would be to challenge the river in the approaching darkness, with Margy becoming more concerned than she already is. There's nothing like a good start, and I'm aware of it. Yet, we're painting ourselves into a corner, running out of time.

*****

AT CONCRETE, JEANNE PULLS OFF ROUTE 20, and heads for the river. As the bridge approaches, I see our first problem. The bridge spans high over the Skagit, and there's no easy place to park and launch the kayak. Then I see the second problem – whitewater.

I know Margy sees the same strong flow, but she says nothing.

"Not a good launch point." I state the obvious.

"No, I'm not going in here," replies Margy matter-of-factly.

I really didn't expect so much whitewater below the bridge. Farther up the river at Rockport or Marblemont such current would be expected, but not at Concrete. Yet there it is.

"You probably noticed the whitewater under the bridge," I state. Duh! "But there's a spot where we could get around it in a gentler flow off to the other side."

"Not going there," says Margy.

"Okay, we'll find a better place," I reply. "Let's get something to eat first, and we'll look at the map."

We drive back to Route 20, where we find the ideal restaurant for our needs. Good food in an atmosphere of days gone by, a diner with a fine menu and a nice table to spread out our chart. It puts us all in a good mood.

"Let's go back down towards Birdsview," I suggest. "We passed several spots that looked good for launching the kayak, and it will be nice to have a shorter paddle to the state park."

"I'm for that," says Margy. "Don't want to be on the river after dark."

So she's been thinking about this, too. No surprise.

"Heck, we can go almost all the way to the park before we put the kayak in the river," I add. "We just need to get our paddles wet today so you feel more comfortable with the rate of flow. It's gonna' be easy."

But it's not going to be easy, and I'm beginning to understand. After ordering a grilled cheese sandwich and lemonade, Margy moves her sandwich back and forth on her plate, but barely nibbles at it. When she eats like this, it's an indication her stomach is in a tizzy. And when she's this quiet, it means she's concerned.

Meanwhile, Jeanne orders a salad and soda, while I tackle the grilled pastrami sandwich and fries. I finish off my meal quickly, Jeanne finishes most of her salad, but Margy eats less than half of her sandwich.

After leaving the restaurant, we head south on Route 20, retracing our path. But Jeanne doesn't slow down when we approach a few potential launch sites, nor do Margy or I speak up as we cruise on through. None of these spots look very good to any of us.

Shortly, we see the sign for Birdsview, which means we're almost back to the state park. Meanwhile, I'm focused on the GPS, giving Jeanne directions for a turnoff that should take us to the end of a riverside road and a potential launch site. We turn down a dirt path that eventually widens to an empty parking area. A sign says "Boat Ramp Closed," a good indicator in the sense that people have actually launched boats here in the past. We don't need a fully functional boat ramp. All we need is clear access to the river. The ramp may be officially closed, but it's the perfect launch site. Better yet, there's no one here to rush us.

We offload the kayak on the downhill-sloping ramp, which makes things easy for Margy's handhold at the bow. We slide *Mr. Kayak* into the Skagit River, and brace the big yellow banana against shore with our extended paddles. There's a mild current here, but in this eddy, nothing seems to be pulling the kayak down river. The kayak merely floats contentedly in the shallow water, ready to go.

We load our gear into the forward and aft hatches, not needing the extra space provided by the center hatch. The straps on the middle

Launch site near Birdsview

hatch are the most cumbersome to deal with, so it's good news that everything fits aboard without needing this compartment. Of course, once we add our camping equipment at Rasar State Park, it may be a different story.

Before packing the soft ice chest in the aft hatch, I remove one of the ice-cube water bottles, now partially melted. I take a swig of the icy water – totally refreshing! – and hand it to Margy.

"Try this," I say. "You won't believe how good this cold water tastes."

We pack an ice bottle next to each of our seats, don our life vests, pull on our water shoes, and put on our gloves. I make one last check of the Tempo's trunk, and we're ready to go. But first I take out my pocket-sized author's notebook and write down a few thoughts about the pending trip. Margy snaps my photo – caught in the act.

"I'll try to get this on video," says Jeanne, as she pulls out her iPhone.

"Okay, but you can expect us to turn around first, and paddle up the river just a little bit," I say. "I want to see how easy it is to make headway upstream, and Margy will feel better then."

Taking notes at Birdsview launch site

I glance at Margy, and she doesn't look so good. But, as usual, she's ready to go without complaint. Of course, we both know this is a gentle spot in a roaring river. But it will give us lots of confidence if we can paddle upstream, even here.

Getting aboard is always the hardest part, but Margy makes a good entrance while I steady the kayak for her. Then she holds her paddle firm against the shore while I step into the rear cockpit. Getting my legs down and my feet onto the rudder pedals is, as always, a challenge. But now we're both aboard and ready to push off. We're on our way!

As soon as we are a few feet from shore, I reach behind me to the rudder bar, and push it full aft. The rudder clangs down.

"Rudder down!" I report.

It's always fun to yell this out when we launch, since it means we're in deep enough water to be fully underway.

I push the left pedal to its maximum travel, and paddle with only my right paddle in the water. Margy does the same with her paddle, and we pivot slowly, headed upriver. The current isn't very strong here, but it's enough to make it difficult to turn, so it's a sloppy uphill paddle. Still, we're going against the current successfully, and I'm sure it makes Margy feel better.

After slogging a few slipshod feet upstream, it becomes increasingly difficult to maneuver in a straight line, so I push the right rudder pedal, and we quickly pivot back downstream. I swear a few choice words as the kayak tries to stabilize itself in heading. Then I remember Jeanne's attempt at some video footage.

"Sorry!" I yell towards the shore.

But I can barely see the launch area now, since we're moving down the river so fast. We get stabilized on track quickly, and down the river we go!

The water under us is wonderfully clear, a green glacier-washed flow. There's a small island directly ahead, with what looks like equal flow to each side. I push the left rudder, and we steer into a narrower flow that's obviously running faster. But there's no whitewater here, and we slip to the side of the island, down and around to the other end where the streams rejoin.

We enter an area of backflow current, but it's easy to navigate through the small white-crested waves. The wind is light and from the west, off our bow, ruffling the water surface further. I ease the rudder enough to point us at a small area of whitewater that seems plenty deep and safe.

"Don't do that!" yells Margy. "Not yet!"

Fair enough. All is going well, and it's only fair to avoid the more challenging parts of the river for now.

"Rocks!" she yells, as we pass over the edge of a small area of whitewater before I can steer back into the smoother flow.

Almost simultaneously, Margy's baseball cap flies rearward in the wind, catches in her long hair, and flops upside down, seemingly in mid-air. She reaches rearward, grabs the hat, pulls it off her head, and throws it determinedly into the cockpit in front of her.

"Damn!" I hear her yell.

When Margy swears like this, she's mighty concerned.

"Plenty deep!" I yell to her from the back cockpit. "The rudder won't even hit."

But I pull the rudder up anyway, not wanting to alarm Margy in case the metal plate bounces off rocks and makes some noise.

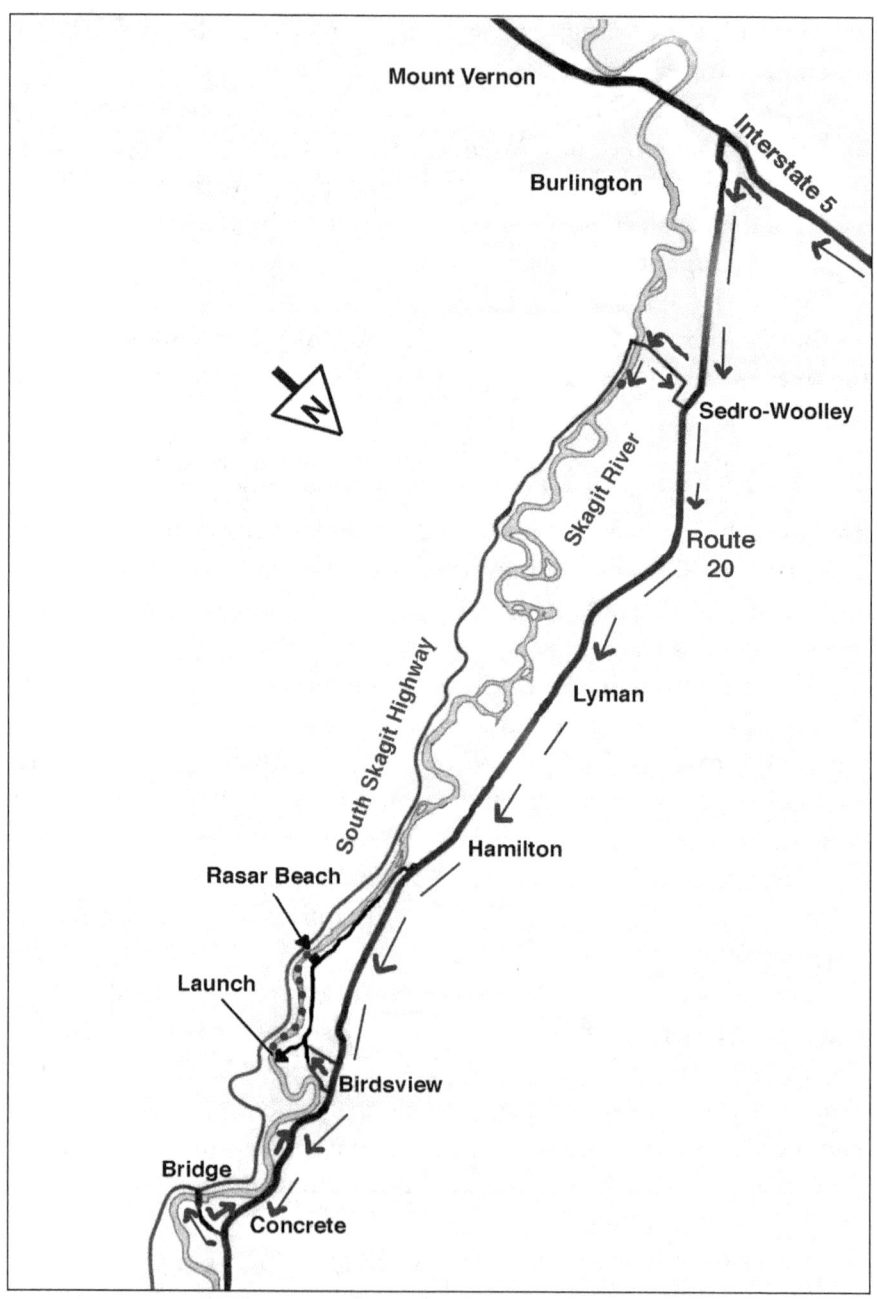

Day 1 on the Skagit River: Birdsview to Rasar State Park

"Rudder's up! I report. "Just in case."
We're back in smooth flow now, and I put the rudder back down.
"Not so bad, is it?" I suggest.
"No, not so bad."
It's going to be alright now. And we both know it.
"Stop paddling for a moment," I say. "Let's see how fast we're going."
I check our GPS speed, and the digital indicator stays fairly steady at 4.7 mph, occasionally increasing to slightly over 5. Throughout the trip, I'll check our speed often, noting maximum non-paddling speeds of up to 9 mph, a nice "pusher." In still water, we're lucky if we can paddle at 5 mph under no-wind conditions. This is what I've been waiting for!

It's only a few miles to Rasar State Park, and I soon see the GPS waypoint coming up on the right side. Rounding the next bend, children are splashing in the water near where we had planned to land. But farther ahead, there's another nice stretch of beach that looks equally adequate for us, right near the trail into the park.

Arrival at beach at Rasar State Park

We pass the batch of kids, and they wave at us enthusiastically. We're quick to return their greeting by flailing our paddles. Then we angle onto the beach and are firmly ashore. No problems – a nearly flawless voyage of at least two full miles. Not much to write home about, but we're thrilled.

As soon as I step out of the kayak, I realize how thirsty I am. With all of the excitement of the launch and first tests in the current, I've completely forgotten to drink any water. It may have been a short stretch of river, but it's at least 90 degrees Fahrenheit, and I'm close to dehydrated by the excitement alone. Similarly, Margy hasn't drunk a drop either since we left Jeanne and the Tempo. I reach back down into my cockpit and pull out the ice-chilled water. It tastes wonderful! Right there on the beach we each drink nearly half a bottle, the best tasting drink I ever remember – followed almost immediately by a swim in the cold refreshing water, not bothering to change out of our shorts and T-shirts. We're in such a hurry to get into the water that we just let the kayak bob without a tether in the shallow water near shore. It jounces up and down within our view, not going anywhere.

The green glacial water is so cold that we have to brave it to get wet up to our necks. But once we're fully in, we can stand it for a few seconds. Then we prance around, ankle deep, just enjoying the cool feeling.

We take some time to carefully pull the kayak completely out of the water, leaving it high enough to be out of reach of any change in flow during the night. Thick bush branches are strong enough to secure the kayak aground for the evening, using our bow and stern lines as safe ties.

With our tent and sleeping gear already at our campsite, there's little to carry back up the trail to the park. So it's a leisurely stroll in the lengthening shadows, still well before sunset. Our water shoes squish as we walk along in our wet clothes, already drying in the warm air.

When we arrive at our campsite, it takes only a few minutes to pitch our tent and prepare ourselves for a glorious first-night after our long-awaited initial probe into the Skagit River.

Campsite at Rasar State Park

Chapter 4

Down the Skagit: Day 2

Skagit River: Rasar State Park to Ross Island WA

The next morning, we bag-drag down to the beach, lugging all of our overnight gear in a single trip. Near our kayak, a fisherman is casting out into the river, using a bright silver lure.

"You've come a long way from Canada," he says with a laugh.

On the stern of our kayak, we fly a small Canadian flag on a tall pole. Along the south shore of British Columbia, boat traffic necessitates that kayakers use caution navigating through the hoard of summer visitors flocking to Desolation Sound each year. Even a big kayak isn't always noticed from the bridge of a fast moving boat, and our flag gives us more confidence that we'll be seen. Plus, we're familiar with the term used by some boaters who operate near kayaks – "speed bumps" is what some of them call us. It's not a particularly endearing term.

"We haven't kayaked all the way down from Canada," I reply. "But that's where the Skagit River originates. Up there in Canada."

"Really?" says the fisherman.

"Yup. Supposedly, there's a lake way up there where the Skagit begins. But we're just headed back home to Canada. We launched near Concrete."

Actually, we launched only two miles upstream, but who's keeping track. For the sake of effect, I sweep my arm down the river, towards the west, where we could (theoretically) paddle into the ocean, then up the coast all the way to British Columbia.

Fisherman at Rasar State Park

The fisherman laughs – an "I'm impressed" chuckle – and continues to cast.

"What kind of fish do you catch here?" I ask.

"Salmon, but you can't keep 'em yet. I'm hoping for a Dolly Varden."

"Now that'd be nice," I reply.

"Steelhead, too," he adds.

I don't have a fishing pole or license on this trip. But you can bet you'll find me fishing on future visits to the Skagit.

When we pile what we've carried next to *Mr. Kayak*, it fits into a small footprint next to the forward and aft hatches without need for the center compartment. Margy rides comfortably with some of our gear in her cockpit, but I need unobstructed floor space because my legs are stretched forward onto the rudder pedals. Still, I keep a small plastic (semi-waterproof) knapsack between my thighs so I can access snacks and gear I need along the way. The GPS is clamped to my life vest, and my camera stands always ready in a hanging waterproof pouch in front of the cockpit.

Arranging camping gear at Rasar State Park

In a few minutes, we're loaded and ready to go. We push off from the beach, with a paddling goal of traveling as far down the Skagit as Ross Island today. This is the biggest island in the river (and the only one named on my GPS), a few miles east of Sedro-Woolley. (The next day, we'll encounter Fir Island in the delta, which is even bigger. But it's an island only because the Skagit splits into its north and south forks as it makes its final run to the sea.)

In this section of the river, current that sounds like waterfalls is announced well in advance. We steer partly by sound to avoid the cascades, but they are not really waterfalls. The swifter water is typically caused by shallow areas where the river runs over rocks or where trees have washed downstream and lodged themselves in the river. We're careful to work our way around the protruding logs, since even a small snag just below the surface could damage our hull. So we avoid spots where water turns white without visible reason. Usually, these below-water snags are announced by the sound of rushing water and a narrow stretch of white.

But there's another reason the whitewater exists, and I prefer to use it to our advantage. Where the river bends, the outside bank runs fast and deep. We could get fun-filled free thrust here, but Margy reminds me she isn't willing to try these spots. So my one regret on this trip is I don't get to experience these less-than-gentle pushers. It's a small price to pay for a paddling companion who is a near-perfect match for my downriver spirit.

"Are you going to help me here?" Margy asks, with a notable tone of concern as we drift towards a patch of whitewater.

As is typical on this trip, I'm kicked back, feet resting gently on the rudder pedals, paddle sitting idle across my lap. Often you'll find me relaxing in the stern compartment, checking my GPS or paper chart, taking photos, or scratching remarks in my author's notebook. Meanwhile, the kayak drifts wherever it wants to go, except for the paddling efforts of Margy and my occasional push on a rudder pedal. Where it wants to go now is towards the swifter current.

As is often the case, I keep fiddling with my gear until the last minute. But with Margy's call to action, I kick the left pedal to help steer us, and Margy digs in a paddle on the right side to establish our track. In the front cockpit, she has less control over our course than I do. Now I've waited so long that it requires quick action to steer us clear of the whitewater. It seems perfectly safe to me, but Margy doesn't see it that way.

"Just let it drift," I say. "We're clear of the strongest current. I'm checking the GPS, but I'll be back with you on the paddles in a minute."

"Now!" she retorts.

"Okay, here we go," I say, quickly putting my GPS back in its case. "But that stretch of whitewater isn't a problem."

"It is to me."

I dig in my paddle on the right side, to make sure she knows I'm finally paying attention. But she has made a good point. I'm constantly ignoring the problem, and she's constantly recognizing it. Once in a while, Margy gives in when I aim towards a seemingly safe section of white that represents a wide shallow bottom near a gravel bar. And sometimes I look down to see rocks directly below – fast moving rocks in the shallow green flow. This kayak needs only a few inches of water, but some situations require retraction of the rudder and a close escape over sharp rocks that could rip the hull.

"Stop paddling, for now, and let it drift through here," I tell Margy. "We don't want to hit rocks at a speed any higher than necessary."

"But we're going crooked," she replies.

"It'll straighten itself out, or let me keep us straight with my paddle. I've pulled the rudder up, and we don't want to go any faster through here."

"So straighten us out!"

Ding! Ding! – a slight tapping on the rocks underneath my seat. Nothing to cause more than a few gentle scrapes of the gelcoat, but a close-enough encounter. If we strike the rocks hard here, travelling slowly, the worst that would probably happen is some hull scrapes and a temporary grounding. From a safety standpoint, we'd then need only to step out into the shallows and push our kayak back into deeper water. No real danger to our bodies, but *Mr. Kayak* could be damaged if sharp rocks are hit at the wrong angle. In other words, Margy is right again.

Which means I'm, well… wrong. Just like when we're flying in our Piper Arrow. She often tempers my airborne enthusiasm in a very positive way. For decades this has kept us out of serious trouble.

Contrary to these brief moments of terror (or slight adrenaline rush, depending on the observer's viewpoint), most of today's ride

Paddling down the Skagit River south of Rasar State Park

is slow and sane, a true gentle pusher that carries us downstream with seldom the need for a paddle. But we paddle, nevertheless, for increased speed and good exercise. Sometimes we paddle together, and sometimes we alternate – a few strokes for me, then I rest while Margy takes over, then me again.

Approaching Hamilton, I hear a noise – *Flop! Flop!*

"Big fish!" I yell.

"I heard it, but didn't see it," says Margy.

"I didn't see it either, but it was definitely a fish. And mighty big."

About 50 feet in front of us, another fish goes airborne, this time clearly visible as a two-foot fish entirely out of the water, then flopping back down.

We've seen only a few fishermen so far, all of them along the gravel bars. As we've passed, I've shouted the same question to shore: "Any luck?" All of the replies have been a sideways shake of the head or a simple yell back: "No!" But big fish are undoubtedly here. This major flopping is proof.

The lack of boats on this river is a surprise to me. I expected to encounter many aluminum boats, even jet boats whose prop-less motors are ideal for this environment, but so far there have been none. Occasionally, along the shore, we see a small boat with an outboard motor, tied up and ready to go, but no other boats move during this part of our trip.

Although there are few homes or cabins to see from our position on the river, I remember the view from the airplane. I know houses are nearby, just out of sight, beyond the narrow tree and brush boundary marking the flood line.

"Where are the recreational boaters?" I ask Margy. "Not just fishermen. Even jet skis would be fun here. They could easily travel up here from the lower parts of the river in conditions like this, perfectly safe since they have no props and can maneuver so easily. I thought we'd see lots of boats."

Neither of us have a proper answer for this. Since a few boats are moored along the shore, powered craft must be legal here. Or maybe they're not allowed during this part of the fishing season. These docked boats might be remnants of earlier months when powered vessels were allowed.

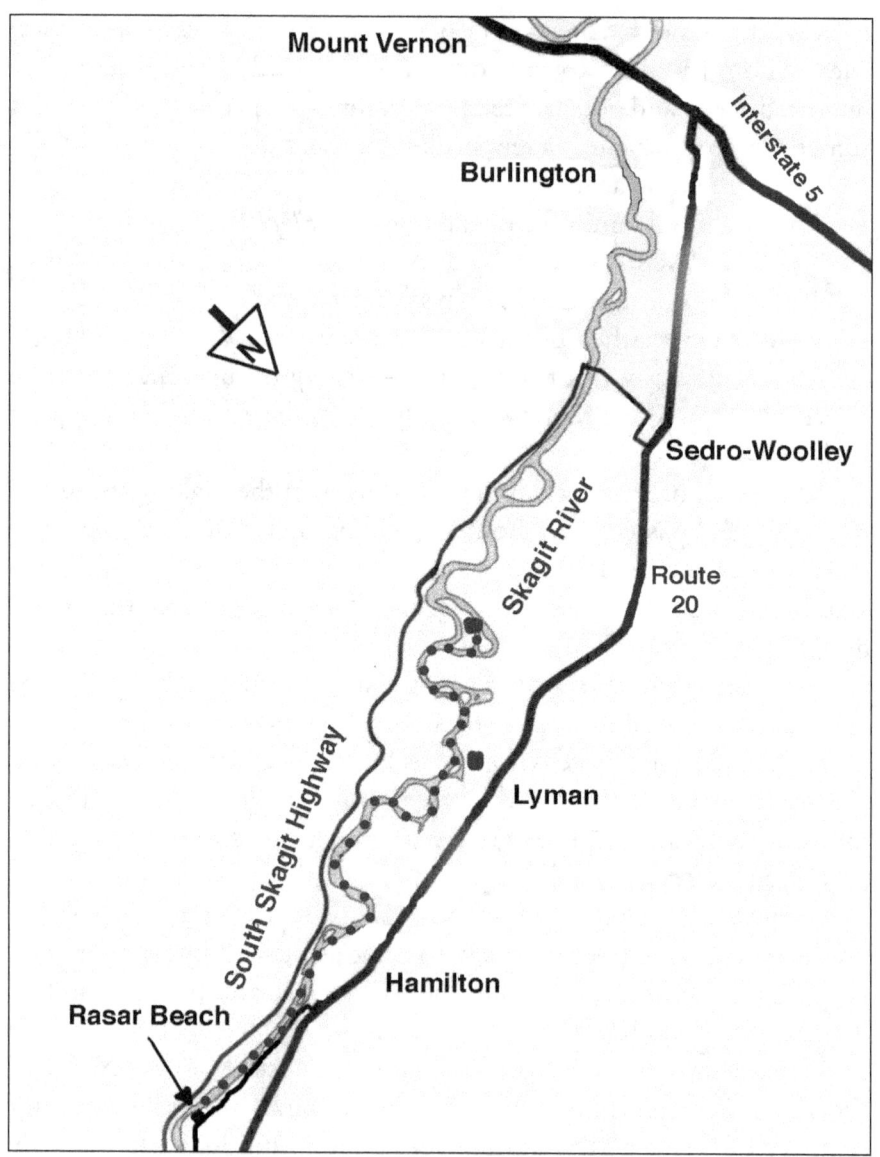

Rasar State Park Beach to Ross Island

Of course, we haven't seen another kayak or canoe either. As far as river vessels go, we're it.

When Hamilton appears off our right side, we find less evidence of the riverside town than expected. My chart shows streets coming nearly down to the water, but little is visible from the river. Margy and I had discussed stopping here or at Lyman for lunch, but I'm not tired yet, still feeling relatively comfortable in the cramped cockpit. Occasionally, I pull my feet off the rudder pedals and stretch them as far forward as possible to prevent cramps, and that technique is working fine so far.

"Want to stop?" I ask.

"How much farther to Lyman?"

"Only 3 more miles."

"Let's keep on going."

Our mutual decision-making is that simple. Once again, this reminds me of how Margy and I make decisions in the cockpit of our Arrow. Even when we're not agreed on our course of action, we make decisions quick and decisively with no regrets. We're onward to the next town.

Just past Hamilton, along the shore, we see a small johnboat, a flat-bottomed aluminum hull designed for fisherman and hunters. It's well adapted to this river, since it's particularly stable, riding over the waves rather than through them. This johnboat with its small Mercury outboard is moored to a small wooden structure that might be considered a dock. No one is nearby, but a green-and-white lawnchair sits on the bank above, as if it's waiting for the owner to return. It's the first of many such chairs along the bank that we'll see

Skagit River approaching Lyman

farther downstream, scenic spots where people just leave their chairs for a return visit and another scenic river view sometime soon.

Approaching Lyman, the river makes a wide U-turn, then west again. The town appears around the next bend, buildings visible in a line along the shore.

The water is shallow near the best-looking spot to bring *Mr. Kayak* ashore. I look for a boat ramp, which you'd think the town would have, but find none. Pulling the kayak out of the water without a sandy beach or ramp, especially when fully-loaded, won't be easy. But there's a deeper area where it seems possible to step ashore and secure the bowline to jutting boulders. We'll let the big yellow banana float while we visit the town.

We climb up the bank, where a gravel road leads to one of the main streets. Then we walk up through the small town, looking for a place to eat.

A small woman with long gray hair to her shoulders is walking along the outside of her wooden fence, watering plants. She inspects us closely as we approach.

"Are you from here?" she asks redundantly, obviously recognizing everyone who lives in this small town.

Parked at Lyman -- Down the Skagit, Day #2

"No, we came down the river in our kayak," I reply.

"A kayak on the river?"

She sounds like it's such an unusual thing. In fact, it sounds like she's surprised there's a river here.

"Great trip," I add. "What a beautiful place."

"Yes, it is," she says. "Came here from Arkansas with my father when I was just a kid. He got a job in the mill."

"What kind of mill?"

"Sawmill. That's all that was here here back then."

We talk for a few more minutes, getting the friendly woman's feel of the town. She says she hardly ever goes down to the river anymore: "After a while, you kinda' forget it's there."

"Is there a place to eat in town?" I ask.

"Not any more," she replies. "Used to be a tavern that served meals, but they're out of business. I used to work there."

"How about up by Route 20?"

"Oh, sure. There's a big place there. Easy walk from here."

When we bid her goodbye, she walks towards her cute little house, where a big satellite TV dish adorns the front porch, pointed low towards the southern horizon where the geostationary satellites are anchored.

We walk another block to the main intersection in town, where the post office and fire station are located. Just up the street, not more than half-a-block is a freshly painted tavern with a bright-looking sign: *Lyman Tavern – the Horniest Tavern in the Northwest.*

"Do you think this is the place she used to work?" I say to Margy. "Must not have been closed for long."

"Seems like it's been kept up pretty good," she replies. "Looks open."

"Isn't that a neon beer sign in the window?" I ask.

We cut across the street, where I pull on the door handle. The door swings open to a spacious restaurant area with a big bar on one end.

"Hello!" says the young woman behind the counter near the cash register. "Come on in."

The woman back at the cute little house never goes over to the river these days. It looks like she never goes one-block into town either.

Mounted deer heads with huge racks explain part of the tavern's claim to it's name of "Horniest Tavern," but the rest of the explanation is the huge neon sign displayed above the bar. You must go there sometime just to see it. Trust me, it's worth the trip.

Although it's only 12:30, this will be our main meal of the day. Margy orders the fried chicken, and I ask for the captain's plate. We have plenty of food here to keep us going all day.

"What brings you to town?" asks the woman as she sets our food on the table. We obviously look like rare tourists.

"Headed down the river in our kayak," says Margy. "We launched near Concrete."

"My husband and I used to do a lot of hunting near Concrete," the woman replies. "But then this guy from Las Vegas bought up all the property, and you can't find a good spot to camp anymore. We thought of buying a spot just to camp, but it didn't work out."

This tweaks my interest, since we've seen several trailers and open lots with picnic tables and small shelters along the river. I thought they were on the backside of a homeowner's property, or even summer squatters, but maybe they were similar spots where locals bought property so they can privately camp.

As we leave the tavern, the young woman's last thoughts are yelled from behind her counter: "Watch out for the logjams between here and Sedro-Woolley."

"We'll do that," I reply.

We've already seen some minor logjams, but they're smaller than we expected. Logjams and "sweepers" (overhanging branches that can sweep a paddler from the boat) are among the hazards listed in the kayak guidebooks, but we've seen few of consequence so far. To us, a logjam is a major blockage of the waterway, as documented in one of my British Columbia books, *Off the Grid* (Chapter 5, "Canoe Route, Kayak Style"). But certainly the woman's advice is worth respecting.

From the tavern, we hike up to Route 20, where there's a large restaurant, gas station, and mini-mart. We buy two jugs of water, radio batteries, and two ice cream bars. On the short walk back to town, I notice a sign on the highway that tells visitors to turn off here for *City Centre* – not much of a city, but a cute little town.

We walk along a nicely groomed grass shoulder of the town's entry road, with no traffic except a green John Deere tractor coming straight at us on the shoulder.

"Here comes the mower," says Margy.

The driver of the tractor, wearing a black baseball cap, stops to let us pass without tossing cut grass at us. He nods and smiles. I nod and smile back. City maintenance, I guess. Welcome to Lyman.

A bit farther along, we try another side street, passing a 1964 Ford Mustang that sits in a dirt turnout by an old house. The red classic, an original Mustang, is different from most I've seen. Of course, it's a rare find, but this one looks like it's active, not just for show. Well worn, a bit dirty, but still in wonderful shape. Somebody in town has an extremely valuable car as their primary source of transportation.

Back at the kayak, we look down the bank at the beauty of this riverside setting. A wide bend and shallow water makes a picturesque scene.

Margy stows the two water jugs we purchased to her front cockpit, so we still haven't used the center compartment on this trip. I pull the kayak forward, and Margy climbs aboard from a flat rock. Then I clumsily hop (flop) aboard, and push off from the ledge.

River view from Lyman

Back on the river, we almost immediately encounter a buildup of logs along the south shore and more in the middle of the river. I point the bow to the right, towards the best available alternative, but the water runs white in a narrow channel near a sandbar. It'll be shallow here, but the kayak should glide over the rocks, at least to my untrained eye.

"Stop paddling!" I yell forward to Margy. "It'll be shallow, and we don't want to scrape at a high speed."

Margy nods her head in acknowledgement. She understands the situation and is ready to face the shallow whitewater as the best choice.

The path is precarious, but there's enough water for the kayak. The rudder brushes the rocks once, so I retract it quickly, sacrificing directional control. Still, we don't need to paddle, as *Mr. Kayak* shifts from side to side in the current, and then steadies straight ahead. It's a good ride in less than 6 inches of green (capped with white) water. When the bottom falls out of sight again, I'm thrilled, and so is Margy.

"Yahoo!" I yell. "The rudder's down again."

"That was fun," replies Margy. "I hate to admit it."

"Pretty soon, you'll be looking for the strongest current, just to keep our speed up."

"I doubt that."

Although it's still early in the day, we decide to try Ross Island as a campsite, if we can find a good place to land. We could easily travel farther downstream, but this may be the end of the secluded part of the river. Pretty soon we'll be gliding past Sedro-Woolley, then I-5 and Mount Vernon.

"We should take the right side around the island," I suggest. "It looks a bit wider."

It makes for an easy decision, especially when Ross Island finally appears in front of us. The turn to the left is stacked with trees, completely impassible. Now, that's a real logjam!

As we pass the clogged area, steering into the wide-open flow to the right, I hear the rush of water under the logjam to our left and into the channel behind it. Just ahead of us on this end of Ross Island seems the perfect spot to camp. Perfect to us means a wide gravel sandbar and a solo fallen log sitting ready to serve as our natural picnic table.

I push the rudder hard left to swing the kayak towards the bar. We make a complete 180-degree turn, facing upriver as we pull up next to the beach. I'm not sure why I want to face this direction, but it makes us look like we know what we're doing.

After removing our camping gear, I'm ready to heft *Mr. Kayak* onto the beach, but Margy has a better idea.

"We could float the kayak down to that log," she says, pointing to a big snag on the beach about 50 feet downstream. "We could tie up there for the night."

There's really no significant change in water level on this part of the river from day to day, but it's a good suggestion. If a big logjam did break loose upstream (or even downstream) the water could rise unexpectedly. So we turn the kayak around in the water (after all of my fancy effort), and walk it down to the area near the log. I lead with the bowline, and Margy stoops down to grab the edge of her cockpit so she can guide the kayak along shore.

"Like herding cattle," she says. "Come along *Mr. Kayak*."

The late afternoon sun is plenty hot, but with a nice breeze, so we hold off pitching our tent, which is always easier in calm conditions.

Skagit River as viewed from Ross Island

Instead, we go for a swim in water that seems colder than back at Rasar beach, probably because the current is swifter here. But it's totally refreshing, and we splash around for quite a while before walking back towards the picnic log and our proposed campsite.

We inflate our air mattresses, and plop them down near the big log in the shade of the trees on the south side. In just a few minutes, I'm on my back, dozing in the shade, while Margy is spread out on her stomach on her mattress reading a book.

"Here come some tubers," says Margy.

"Huh?" I say a bit deliriously, still almost asleep.

"Tubers. On real inner tubes."

To me, tubers are people who ride behind powerboats on Powell Lake, a wimpy alternative to waterskis. Such tubes are typically big, elaborately adorned with handholds, and constructed of bright-colored plastic. Margy is talking about old-fashioned tire tubes with valve stems poking out.

As sleepy as I am, I want to see this. It's our first encounter with anyone floating on the river in a vessel of any kind, but I doubt it will be our last. After all, we're rapidly approaching a more densely populated area.

By the time I prop myself up on an elbow, two tubers have already passed us, but there's two more coming. The first two are yelling back to us or maybe to their buddies: "Canadians!"

Our tall Canadian flag is a dead giveaway. And I suppose it looks a bit strange in these waters.

"No paddles or nothing," says Margy. "Just using their hands to splash around and keep their direction."

The next two tubers make a grand arrival. They ground themselves right next to *Mr. Kayak*, stand up (staggering), and are looking the kayak over closely. Being a bit nervous about this, I start to get up and walk over to them. But they beat me to it, by heading directly towards Margy and me.

"Hey, Canadians!" yells the young man, who wears only blue baggy shorts and black water shoes. His skinny but cute girlfriend, dressed in only a skimpy bikini and no shoes is riding piggyback, coming straight at us.

"It's those crazy American!" I shout back.

I hold out my hand, and introduce Margy and myself. His name is Tim, and she's Dana.

"Where are your shoes?" I ask the girl, still perched on Tim's shoulders.

"I had them when we started," says Dana. "But they got lost somewhere along the way."

"Crazy Americans," I reply. "So what do you have with you, besides your tubes?"

"Beer, of course," says Dana. "It's in my pack back at the tubes."

Plus a cell phone that's been ringing nearly constantly since he pulled it out of his pocket (waterproof, I hope), after setting Dana down. Tim ignores the ring while we're talking, waits for it to stop, then opens the phone.

"Man, eight voicemail messages," he says.

Then he closes the phone, ignoring the messages, and tells us about their trip. I hope mom and dad aren't frantic.

Arrival of the Crazy Americans

Dana and Tim have floated down the river from Lyman, so they must have departed shortly after us. We've been here only a few hours, and their trip, without paddles, must have taken longer. They live in Lyman and plan to pull out of the water at Sedro-Woolley, along with their two friends now well ahead of them.

"So will you come ashore at the boat ramp at the San Pedro RV Park?"

"That's Sedro-Woolley," corrects Margy. "San Pedro is in Los Angeles."

"Close enough," I laugh. "Almost the same thing."

"We might meet our friends in front of us," says Tim. "Not really sure. They may be worried about us now, because we've got the beer."

"So how will you get back to Lyman?" I ask.

"We know some people in Sedro-Woolley, so we'll find a ride."

Hot summer day, inner tubes on the river, no real plans. Ah, youth!

We walk back to the Crazy Americans' tubes, Dana once again on Tim's back. Dana's smaller tube has a giant bulge that looks like it's about to pop. Tim's beer is in a backpack he wears facing forward on his chest so they can get at the refreshments without leaving the river.

"Careful there," I say to Dana, pointing at the metal-tipped valve stem with no plastic cap. "That could hurt."

Tubers depart the beach

She laughs, slides her tube into the shallow water, and plops down into her small cocoon, missing the protruding stem by only an inch. Tim pushes his bigger tube into the water beside Dana's, and slides down into it. Dana splashes to turn her tube, and they lock their feet together.

"This is how we keep together during the trip down the river," says Tim. "We swing like a Ferris wheel, bumping off logs as we go."

Margy would definitely not like traveling like this. Those cell phone messages that Tim ignored were definitely their parents.

Once Tim and Dana have departed, we hear them screaming as they hit the next rapids around the corner. By now Tim is probably reaching for a beer.

Margy and I go for another quick dip, just to cool off before pitching our tent. Then we walk back to the log to sit and dry off. A big fish jumps completely out of the water on the opposite shore, coming down with a resounding plop. It's a fitting ending to a wonderful day on the river.

Campsite at Ross Island

◊ ◊ ◊ ◊ ◊ ◊

Chapter 5

Down the Skagit: Day 3
Skagit River: Ross Island to Conway WA

Early the next morning, we sit on our log, eating fruit cups and snack bars, drinking orange juice from sealed cartons. The first boat we've seen in motion on the river arrives from downstream, blasting up through the current with apparent ease. This is a 20-foot aluminum johnboat, flat-bowed and powered by a hefty-looking outboard, probably a jet drive, with two people and fish poles hanging out the sides. They stop just above our campsite, near the big logjam blocking the other side of Ross Island. I watch them tie up to a log that angles up and out of the river, and they begin to fish. (I later learn that one of the regulations regarding fishing on this river involves no fishing while under engine power.)

The johnboat is still above our location when we push off Ross Island for the last day of our trip. Herons along the sandbar near our campsite scatter in honor of our departure, and I hear an eagle screech on the other shore. We almost immediately encounter some rough water, but we navigate around the edge of it.

"Is this the right way?" asks Margy, as we begin our turn at a split in the river that's not on the map. "It looks like a dead end."

"Seems good," I reply. "It looks a bit wider on this side, and the current is still running, so it must rejoin the other stream."

"Must be the right way," she says. "Because here comes the boat."

The aluminum johnboat slows a bit, gives us a wide berth, and passes, now returning downstream. The two fishermen wave, and we wave back. They stop a short distance below us, and tie their bow to

Logjam near Ross Island

another snag, Their bow swings upriver, their boat pulled downstream on their short rope, fish poles out the stern.

There are more logjams now, extensive logs lodged in the river and bigger piles along the shores. But it's still far from the blockage I imagined. We hear the logjams as we approach, noisy current around the flows, so they're easy to avoid. Just past a major jam, the johnboat from upstream passes us again, headed farther downstream.

Roads run along both sides of the river, all the way from Concrete, but the southern road is now discernible right along the water. Houses and cabins also become more plentiful, as seen from the river. They've probably been there all along, but now they're visible right on the banks. More lawn chairs, some solo and others side-by-side, sit on the edge of the river, here and there, along with still more private-looking campsites. Some of the sites include a camper trailer, while others are vacant except for a picnic table and a covered sitting area.

We pass a major sign of inhabitation, a large cabin with a boat launch ramp adjacent. Our two johnboat fishermen are working around their boat at the ramp, preparing to pull it onto its trailer. Suddenly one of the fellows bursts into loud song.

"Oh, Canada!" He gets right into the main chorus of the Canadian national anthem, singing it with perfect annunciation. He goes through the whole anthem while we drift by, and we give him encouragement by our cheers. I'd like to join him in the verse, but I don't really know the words. He does.

The north shore now has regularly-spaced homes, but most are partially covered from view by trees along the banks. About a mile farther along, still another man bursts into "Oh, Canada!" But he struggles and stumbles over the words, just like a real Canadian. He hums through some of the verse, and we cheer him on. Maybe it's time to take our flag down.

"There's the Sedro-Woolley launch ramp," I say to Margy as we pass.

"Don't you mean San Pedro?"

"Of course," I reply. "No need to stop, eh?"

"No, let's keep going," says Margy. "But we could make it to shore, if we wanted to. The river doesn't seem to be moving so fast from out here. From the shore it looked horrible."

The crisis has mostly passed, and Margy has settled into real enjoyment of the changes in flow. Around one bend in the river I actually hear her say: "Let's slip over into the current a bit."

We're slowing noticeably now. I dip a finger into the water and taste it. Still no salt, nor even a sign of brackishness. But we've now entered the tidal influence, which extends all the way inland to Sedro-Woolley. By our good fortune (but I call it perfect timing), the ocean flow is now slowing as the turn to ebb tide is now approaching. In another two hours, we'll be in full downstream flow. The outward flow of the river towards the ocean, coupled with a retreating tide, should make the lower portion of our journey easy. As guidebook accounts indicate, during a flooding tide, we would need our paddles to get very far past Sedro-Woolley.

At a wide sandbar below the old classic Sedro-Woolley Bridge, we're ready for a break. We spot a log on the gravel bar that can act as a seat and picnic table, and we head for it. We slip gently to shore, and pull the kayak halfway out of the water. On the inviting log in the sun, we sip on juice and snack on peanut butter encased by crackers.

Paddling break below Sedro-Wooley

My back is beginning to hurt, a malady that seems to occur only in a kayak, so I'm glad to be on shore. On my first ride in a single-person kayak in Canada, I needed Margy's help to get back to our rental location in Okeover Inlet. My back was so sore that I needed to tow me the last few kilometers. It's a sport where Margy's physical abilities outshine mine. My inflatable seatback support helps a lot, but today my back is approaching its limit. And after several hours with my feet on the pedals, my cramped legs seek relief.

At the beach, I ask Margy if she minds swapping life vests. I notice that hers seems to ride a bit lower in the back, and it may provide me with some relief against top of the seat and the rear lip of the cockpit. So we exchange vests, but once we're underway again, it seems to make little difference.

After departing the gravel bar, we encounter a series of bridges, some structured in old, handsome metal, others molded of stark modern concrete. Roads and railroad tracks cross the river, and we aim

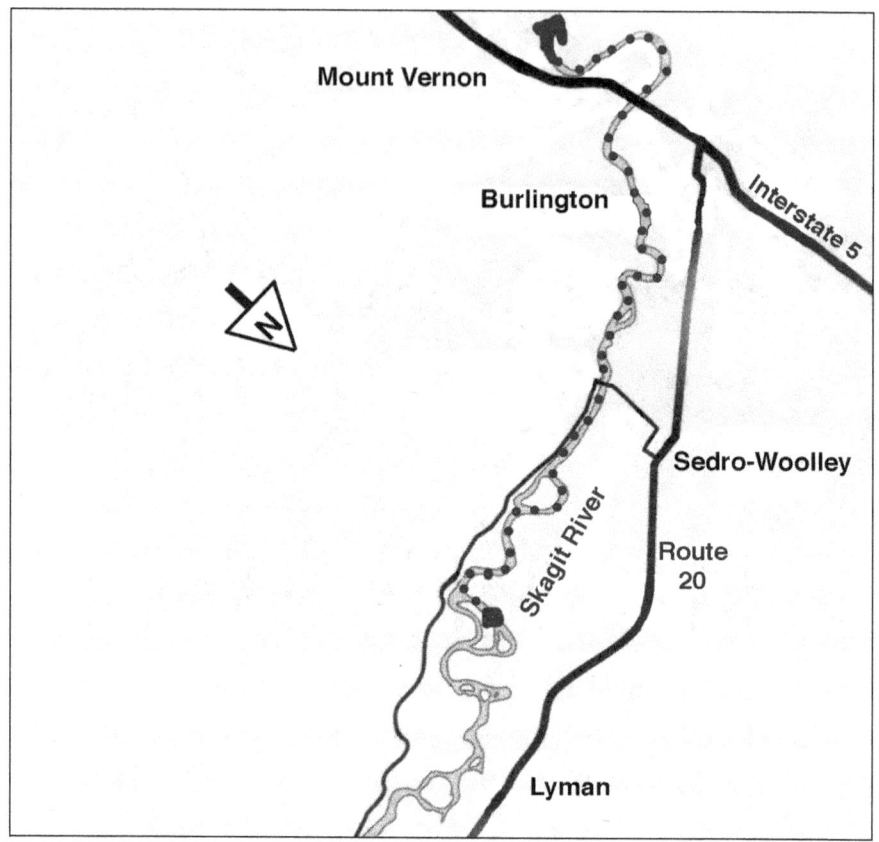

Day #3: Ross Island to Conway Bridge (lower Skagit River)

for the opening between the pilings where logjams are minimal. The pillars on the upstream side are a popular place for logs to congregate.

A big milestone is ahead – the Interstate-5 bridge. First there's a modern concrete road over the river, then the less impressive I-5 crossing.

Before this, we pass a private marina, where a gated dock and old-design hardtop boats sit on several dock fingers. These vessels are classic-looking, and all seem to be in port today. Why is there so little boat traffic on this river, especially down here where the flow is slower and deeper?

"Look! A kite!" I yell to Margy, as a white object shoots nearly straight up from beyond the marina gate, behind the tall rocks of the riverbank.

"It's a model airplane!" she shouts back.

The big model aircraft climbs nearly vertically, then rolls at the top, before beginning a wide turn and a slow descent. I'm not sure what's beyond the bank of rocks, but now everything is looking more artificial. The shore is lined with staged rows of big rocks, a sturdy-looking dike for a river that's prone to flood in the spring.

My finger taste test in the water still reveals a lack of brackishness. In fact, all the way to our eventual pullout at Conway, the water remains fairly fresh in my tests. The river is still green and clean, but notably slower, and no more islands.

Past the concrete bridge that foreshadows I-5, we watch big trucks scream over the interstate bridge, passed by faster cars, then a horse trailer, and a bus in one of the opposing lane of the interstate. The visual calamity of civilization, and the clamor of hoards of vehicles, all going somewhere.

I-5 is composed of four lanes here, two in each direction. From the river, we will look up to see vehicles seemingly a few feet apart flowing in close file at a terrific speed, a ear-pounding noise above us. For me, it's the most terrifying part of the whole trip. Returning to this fast-paced environment is too noisy and sudden.

We're under the I-5 bridge for only a few seconds, but I'm relieved to come out the other side. The noise fades slowly behind us, and I'm grateful. (Later, in 2013, this section of the bridge collapses when hit by an oversized trailer. Traffic between Seattle and the Canadian border is disrupted by major detours for a full month.)

Beyond Interstate-5, the river is still beautiful, although somewhat industrial off to the sides, with occasional buildings and tall tanks protruding above the embankment. We pass through a residential area, with the tops of houses visible here-and-there above the tall levees.

"It feels like a wide canal through here," says Margy.

And it does. There are only a few pockets of remaining whitewater, and the banks along the sides are mostly artificial concrete and rock slopes. I check our GPS speed – 2.5 miles per hour now, but we push it up to 5.0 with a little paddling.

On this portion of the Skagit, small booth-like sheds are located along the banks, each with a set of stairs down from the tiny huts to a small dock or just a flattened patch of gravel. I don't see any boats here, but it sure looks like a fishing shed and boat launch. Or maybe fishermen just stand below these little buildings and cast for salmon. At the big bend in the river below I-5, I count four sheds in a brief stretch of a half-mile.

Large flights of geese have been traveling up and down the lower reaches of the river all day, and one flock passes in front of us now. If it weren't mid-summer, I'd suspect these were migrating birds. But there's no directional trend in their movements. I've watched them for the last few hours, moving this way, then that, landing on the river and taking off again in a different direction.

A wide U-turn takes us back towards I-5 and the city of Mount Vernon. Ahead along the left bank are tall buildings, with the interstate rushing alongside. Another turn to the right, and a wide gravel beach comes into view. People are far out into the water on this warm afternoon. Children play in the sand, and families congregate in shaded areas closer to the bank of the river.

We notice a spot in still water just beyond the end of the gravel bar and we head into this small, shallow bay. There's a sizable log to tie up to, and from here, we'll be able to walk up to the street and find a restaurant near the bridge for lunch.

Beachfront park at Mount Vernon, Day #3

A young couple is spread out on a blanket nearby in the shade of the trees. There's lots of activity here, and I'm a bit uncomfortable leaving the big yellow banana without my attention.

"Would you mind watching our kayak?" I say to a young fellow with a trimmed goatee.

"Sure," he says. "Where'd you come from?"

Canadian flag, Canadian hat. Here we go again.

"From Concrete," I reply. "Started two days ago. Great river."

"I'm from Concrete," he says.

Small world. The international world of the Skagit.

"I'm really not worried about the kayak," I state. "If kids want to look it over, that's fine. Just don't let anyone sail away with it. Unless it's you."

He laughs, and I feel comfortable to have asked for his help.

Margy and I scramble up the rocky bank to the dirt parking lot, then walk the short distance to the street where the bridge crosses. We bear right, and find a fine looking Mexican restaurant across the street that should be ideal for our appetites.

The comfortable dining room at Las Coronas is empty, so the young waiter suggests we take a booth of our choice. Since no one else is here, I use Margy's cell phone to call Jeanne right from our table.

"We're in Mount Vernon now," I report. "We're in a restaurant eating lunch, and then we'll be headed towards the lower delta. So I'd estimate we'll be pulling out of the river in another 2 hours. I'll call from the river when we get closer to our pullout point, but let me give you directions to the spot now."

I read her the driving instructions from the guidebook that sound like an easy exit from I-5, straight across the Fir Island Bridge at Conway, then left to the Skagit Wildlife Recreation Area. I had originally planned to exit the river at the bridge near Conway, but now Margy and I are planning to go farther down the south fork. What I don't notice is the scale on the guidebook map has changed on the page covering the Fir Island region. It's farther to our pullout point than I think. Add to this the slowing flow of the river, and we're now behind schedule, though we don't know it yet.

And there's one other minor error. I gloss over the instructions from the guidebook regarding the I-5 exit, regarding taking a double right to get to the Fir Island Bridge. It looks like a pretty straightforward exit, and surely there are signs to Fir Island.

"Just let me know," she says. "The Tempo is ready for the job."

Back at the river park, I thank the goateed man, and we launch quickly. We glide under the bridge and past the big wharf that lines the other side of the river. I place another call to Jeanne, giving her an estimate of a little over an hour to our proposed pullout.

"I'll be on my way in just a few minutes," says Jeanne.

We paddle through slower water now, finally making the left turn at the split in the river. Now we're on the South Fork, but progress is slow. I check the GPS, and the Fir Island Bridge is farther away than expected.

"I'm getting tired," I say to Margy. "How about you."

"I'm okay, but we can stop at the bridge instead. We should be able to catch Jeanne on her cell phone before she gets off I-5."

"We're way behind schedule now, so I'm gonna' call her."

There's no answer, but Jeanne may be out of the cell coverage area. Besides she doesn't feel comfortable answering the phone in the car, and it's not legal in Washington without a hands-free setup. So I leave a voicemail, instructing her to stop before she crosses the Fir Island Bridge and look for us off to the right.

We pass two boats small boats, both headed up the river. The number of vessels we've seen in three days is minimal. Yet this looks like an ideal boating area, to say nothing of fishing.

It seems to take forever to get to the bridge, but finally we're there. The launch ramp is tucked in tight below the bridge, and we don't see it until we're almost on top of it. Then it's an easy landing, where another kayak (probably coming up from the delta) is being removed from the water and put on the top of a car. By the time we're against the shore, the ramp is ours, but we decide to pull out of the way and unload *Mr. Kayak* before dragging it up the ramp. It could be a bit of a wait for Jeanne, so we'll gather our gear and be ready to pull the boat out when she arrives. If we're lucky, the ramp will stay unoccupied until she shows up, which will mean a simple lift onto the Tempo right at the water.

I phone Jeanne again to make sure she received my message to stop at the Fir Island Bridge. Once again, my call goes to her voicemail. In

Pullout under the Conway Bridge

a few minutes she calls me back.

"Where are you?" I ask.

"Don't really know. I've been driving a long way since I got off I-5."

"That sounds wrong," I say. "You should have gone through Conway and then seen the bridge. That's where we are."

"I haven't seen any bridge," she says. "Lots of cows though. Whew, do they stink. Wish I could roll this window up, but it's jammed half-down."

"Wait a minute," I say. "Maybe you're headed towards Milltown."

"Could be. All I know is there isn't any bridge, and I've driven for miles."

Finally we agree she should go back to the interstate exit, and start all over. This takes another twenty minutes, and you can blame it on me. I should have told her about the double right turn.

But soon we're all reunited under the bridge: Tempo, big yellow banana, and all three of us. It marks the end of the best kayak trip I've ever experienced. So far.

◊ ◊ ◊ ◊ ◊ ◊

Chapter 6

The Complicated Simple Life
Fishing the Lower Skagit and Upper Nooksack

A friend has described my lifestyle at my Canadian home as "the complicated simple life." He's right.

Traveling to my floating home from the United States is, in itself, a complicated process. First I must enter Canada, clearing the border and then either driving to Powell River (which requires two ferries) or flying into the small city's airport. Then I proceed to the marina on Powell Lake, where I transfer to my boat for the voyage up the lake. There's no access to my floating home except by boat.

Once at the cabin, I'm in an off-the-grid setting in every sense of the phrase. I produce electricity using solar power, wind, and a thermoelectric generator on my wood stove. I fill my sink by an old-fashioned hand pump rather than a fancy pressurized faucet. An outhouse serves as a bathroom (recently replaced by a "modern" compost toilet), and bathing in tub is by the old cowboy method: pour a bucket of woodstove heated water over your head. All groceries are packed in by boat, and trash is packed out the same way. Since I need occasional services in town (such as the Internet), I travel back and forth to civilization by boat and then truck – the complicated simple life.

It's in my nature to cherish such a lifestyle. I find it exciting, though demanding. Peaceful, although sometimes I jump too fast from one pace (remote living) to another (city-folk comforts). When I'm in the U.S., I tend to continue with a complicated simple life that keeps me moving. Paddling kayaks in the States is an example, as evidenced by my first river adventure in an alternate kayak.

Floating cabin at Hole in the Wall, Powell Lake, BC

The "complication" involving this new kayak begins when I decide to try my hand at fishing in the State of Washington. That first trip down the Skagit made me realize I was missing an opportunity to experience fishing in a river known for big fish – salmon, steelhead, bull trout, and even Dolly Varden. The next time I tackle the rivers of the area, I'd be ready.

While Margy and I plan our next kayak outing, I purchase a freshwater license and gear appropriate for big river salmon. At Wholesales Sports in Burlington, I talk to a salesman about what I'll need, and he shows me the typical Skagit setup – a y-swivel connecting my line to a small lure on a three-foot leader and a sinker on a short extension.

"Doesn't look like much," he says, pointing to a silver Dick Nite spoon. "But you can throw it a good ways with the sinker, and it's what just about everybody uses on the Skagit."

"It's for fishing from shore?" I ask.

"Or from a boat tied up to a logjam. Just cast downstream, and wait for the salmon to hit."

"What about in a kayak? Can I just drift, and pull the rig along?"

Now that I think about it, I'm not sure you can drift troll on the Skagit. Motorized trolling is illegal, I'm pretty sure, so I'll probably have to tie up to a stump."

"Probably too fast in that current," he replies. "You could throw an anchor overboard."

Who carries an anchor in a kayak? Besides, in the Skagit, wouldn't an anchor be prone to snag on an underwater log? I visualize myself cutting the anchor rode on my first attempt.

"How about a bucket?" I ask. "I could throw one overboard. That should slow me down."

The salesman looks doubtful, but I've used this technique in my tin boat on Powell Lake for trolling slower than my outboard motor normally allows at minimum throttle.

"Maybe, but I think you'd still be traveling too fast," he says. "Try tying up to a snag instead."

Good idea. And the game warden might prefer it.

Leaving the store in Burlington, I decide to try my new rig at the Skagit boat ramp at the end of Gardner Road, only a few miles away. It's the second week of salmon season on this section of the river, so the easily accessible bank north of the ramp is full of anglers, all of them cast out with rigs that probably resemble the one I plan to use. This is Dick Nite territory.

I find a spot a little farther upstream, slightly removed from the crowded bank. It's a muddy trudge, but it looks promising. Ignoring the salesman's recommendation regarding rigging, I try casting with only the small Dick Nite lure, but it's too light to get any distance. So I change to one of my standard trout lures, a heavier speckled yellow spoon that should be as good as anything. My lazy fisherman theory is that fish will bite anything if they're in the mood. If they're not in the mood, they won't bit anything.

On my third cast, I snag something at the bottom of the muddy river, and then work the lure around up and down the shore, trying to free it. After a few minutes, I conclude that it's hopeless, and give my pole a solid tug until the line snaps. Then I switch to the more elaborate Dick Nite triangular rig with sinker, which looks like it will snag even more easily on the bottom.

Sure enough, I lose my lure and sinker, and rig up another. After losing that, too, I conclude there's a reason the other fishermen are all lined up together on the wide bank farther downstream. They must know about the hidden snags in this inviting-looking stretch.

I enjoy fishing, but I don't enjoy spending excess time at a fishing spot. I figure if you don't catch anything on the first few casts, the location is dead. And if you lose your rig three times in fifteen minutes, it's time to quit.

* * * * *

I DRIVE FARTHER UP ROUTE 20, stopping at prospective fishing spots along the way. Using a trout lure, I cast my line, and reel back in quickly, preventing my hook from sinking into the invisible obstacles lurking below the surface. Above Hamilton, I discover a parking spot right near a deep pool that demands my attention. Although I don't experience a single bite, there's no doubt this is a fishing spot requiring another visit. Fishing calls to you like that.

Although the results have been negative by most standards, I'm pleased I now know more about fishing this river. Sometimes you learn more by just getting out there and doing it. I'm ready for the next step – fishing from my kayak.

* * * * *

THINGS GET COMPLICATED, but this time it's not my fault. Margy's mom ends up in the hospital in Bellingham, and our next planned kayak trip on the lower portion of the Nooksack is delayed indefinitely. The early October weather is perfect for a river trip, but I can't do it myself. For one thing, I'd look awkward and conspicuous in the big yellow banana all by myself. It's a mighty big kayak, and the bow lifts way out of the water with me solo in the back where the rudder pedals are accessible. Besides, there's slim hope of my lifting the kayak off the car by myself, and getting it back on the roof racks seems entirely out of the question without a second person to assist. (In fact, these obstacles are later solved, but for now I'm looking at defeat. See Chapter 15, "Go North, Young Man," for a method to load a big kayak onto a car single-handedly.)

So I no longer contemplate a river trip, but I can still fish from the shore. So I decide to try the upper reaches of the Nooksack.

When I'm in Bellingham, I drive a small two-seat car that Toyota produced for a few years before realizing few drivers wanted a gutless sports car. Yet it suits me fine, sliding the top down to get a feel of the outdoors at highway speed. It's the perfect vehicle to take a friend for a drive on a winding country road on a sunny day, or I can use it to pick up some groceries around town. Just don't try to do both at the same time. In other words, it's the perfect one-person convertible, so I'll use it for today's fishing trip to the upper north fork of the Nooksack River.

I study the route in my GPS, finding a bridge in a remote location that seems perfect. The right side of my Toyota two-seater is loaded with fishing gear, including high rubber boots, foul-weather gear, and plenty of lures. Fortunately, my fishing pole is collapsible, since it's the only kind that comfortably fits in this car.

I drive out Route 532, the Mount Baker Highway, passing over the Nooksack's main fork at Deming, and then up along the north fork. I exit on Mosquito Lake Road, which takes me to the bridge, where I find good access in a pullout area with a trail down to the river. To me, this looks like the perfect fishing spot.

Another fisherman is already at the shore, his pickup truck parked next to the concrete piling below this side of the bridge. It's a vehicle that has probably made its way down the trail quite easily. But a truck is a lot heftier than my puny Toyota two-seater. The fisherman stands near his truck, fishing in the most perfect looking river I've seen in a long time. Narrower and swifter than the Skagit, this is the kind of river I've dreamed about kayaking. But the big yellow banana isn't the best vessel for such a river, and Margy would feel particularly uncomfortable paddling in this challenging environment. I know her personal limits in the water, and this is beyond them. Besides, she won't be available for kayaking for a while. So it's a visual dream that stands beyond reality. Still, it's a nice river trip to contemplate. If only I could do it myself in a smaller kayak.

There's a vague hint here of something I'm missing, but at the moment it doesn't strike me. Instead, I let my thoughts slide away from running the river in a kayak, and consider why I've come here today – to fish from the shore.

There's plenty of room for two fishermen along this section of the river, so I walk downstream on the gravel bar a few hundred feet and rig up my pole. I again try a Dick Nite without a sinker, which is a simple direct rig. But the spoon is too light to get any casting distance. So I switch to a heavier rooster tail lure instead. With it, I can cast almost all the way to the other side of the river, where whitewater runs against the steeply banked shore. I cast upstream at a 45-degree angle, and let the lure ride downstream until it's 45-degrees behind me. Then I wind back in, feeling the rooster tail tap the rocky (but seemingly snag-free) bottom. If there are trout or salmon here, this seems like a good way to attract them.

But nothing bites, so I walk farther down the gravel bar, where a creek comes in from the left, producing an even more ideal-looking fishing spot. As is often the case, I find exquisite surroundings I thoroughly enjoy, without catching any fish. But under these circumstances, you'll never hear me complaining. I'm a guy who fishes more for the thrill of the outdoors than the catch. It's a good thing, since my fishing record is definitely not stunning.

When I walk back upstream, the pickup truck is gone, but another fisherman now stands in a perfect-looking pool near the opposite side of the bridge. His big black Labrador Retriever runs back and forth along the shore, enjoying the outing. The fisherman yells something I can't understand in the noise of the whitewater along his side of the river, but I guess he's asking the typical question: "Any luck?"

"Nothing!" I yell back, simultaneously motioning laterally with my arm.

He nods in understanding. Then, only a few minutes later, he latches onto a big fish. When he pulls it into his net, I can see it's at least two feet long, maybe a salmon.

"What is it?" I yell.

"Bull trout!" he yells back.

Bulls look very similar to Dolly Vardens, except for a slight difference in their dorsal (top) fin. So far, I've not caught either species, but I'd love to catch a legendary Dolly Varden someday.

I cast here a few more minutes, long enough for the fisherman on the other side to leave. Then I try casting all the way across to the pool where he caught the trout. I can't quite reach the spot from this side, but I do manage to get hung up on an underwater snag and lose my lure. It's time to quit. (There's a trend here, in case you haven't noticed.)

I walk back up to my car, using my remote control to unlock the doors as I approach. I don't like the way the car alarm chirps. It's almost the normally-expected sound, but unusually faint. I think I know what this means, and it ain't good.

My small two-seater is driven only a few days each month, sometimes even less often. And the battery goes dead when I leave the vehicle inoperative for long periods of time. But I'm used to recharging the battery before I use the vehicle, and this week has been no different. I recharged the battery a few days ago, when it wouldn't crank after sitting in the garage for six weeks. Since then it has started just fine. Of course, now I'm way up the Nooksack, with no one nearby to assist. So the writing seems to be on the wall, but I refuse to face it.

Instead of trying to start the car, I decide to relax and have a snack. I slide back the convertible roof and sit in the driver's seat in the shade of a huge maple tree. I munch on a chocolate-coated granola bar and sip on a boxed orange juice, avoiding the inevitable. Maybe if I ignore the situation, it'll never materialize.

I take my time pulling off my boots and putting on my shoes. After stowing my fishing gear, I finally settle back and prepare to engage the starter.

Click-click.

Nothing more than *click-click*. The battery is dead.

I can try to walk down the road to find a house, or I can wait until someone comes along the road, and flag them down. But instead, I decide to hike back down to the river and enjoy a few more quiet moments by the river before I engage in the expected commotion. It's a good attitude for the moment, and I'm proud of it.

When I reach the concrete pier of the lower bridge, I look downstream. On my side of the river about a hundred feet away is a fly fisherman, casting out into the river. Where did he come from?

As I walk towards him, the man's back is turned away from me, watching his fly drifting downstream. I'm hoping he'll turn around so I don't sneak up on him unexpectedly. But he continues facing downstream, so I walk up within a few feet of him and management an awkward "Howdy!" that gets his attention. He turns to me with a surprised and questioning look.

"I'm sorry to bother you," I say to him, as if I've just walked up to him at the supermarket. "But I've got a weird problem I hope you can help me with."

"What's that?" he asks, looking at me with a suspicious eye.

I stand there without a fishing pole, loafer shoes, shorts, and a tourist-like T-shirt emblazoned with: *I Fly for Food*.

"Well, I'm parked up there, by the road, and my battery is dead. I don't suppose you have a vehicle nearby that might have a set of jumper cables."

"Let's see," he replies, motioning to the woods near the base of the bridge. "I'd say there's about a hundred percent chance of that."

When I look towards where he points, I see the glint of a dark green SUV parked in a side-trail leading down from the area where my Toyota is parked, although I didn't notice it earlier. Meanwhile, he's been downstream all this time, and has just now returned to the bridge.

"Oh, good. What a break," I say, stumbling over the words. "Just take your time, and finish your fishing. I'll be up there when you drive out."

"Okay."

I'm not sure whether I should stay and talk some more or just leave. After all, I've provided a major interruption in this man's fishing experience. So I simply turn and leave.

Back at my car, I sit and wait only a few minutes before the fisherman drives up the hill to assist me. My day has gone strangely. I travel to a remote fishing location, end up with a dead battery in the middle of nowhere, and find almost instantaneous help. Maybe this place is trying to tell me something.

After jumping my battery and profusely thanking the fisherman, I drive back to Bellingham, thinking through what has happened today (and this week). My kayak trips with Margy in the big yellow banana have changed from exciting anticipation to a screeching halt. I've found the type of river I've dreamed of, have learned about the fishing gear to accompany such a trip, but I don't have a usable kayak.

That's when the idea hits me. Crossing the bridge on Route 532 where the main branch of the Nooksack tumbles down towards the sea,

I look upstream. Several fishermen, taking advantage of the opening of salmon season only a few days ago, are standing in knee-deep water. I could be running this river in a kayak, enjoying the swift current and stopping to fish in spots otherwise inaccessible. I have the necessary fishing gear and every piece of kayaking equipment that's required, except for the right vessel. All I need is a single-seat kayak to go with all my gear. It's an idea that's developed in spurts today, occasionally coming to the surface and nearly announcing itself. The complicated simple life is sending out germinating messages.

Before Highway 532 merges into Sunset Boulevard, I remember standing in the fishing department at Wholesale Sports yesterday, watching a young woman investigating a small kayak propped up in the camping department, right next to the spot where I was inspecting fishing lures. Now I even remember the big sign: *All Kayaks, 30% Off.* Now there's a bargain.

* * * * *

I DON'T NEED MUCH OF A KAYAK. After all, this is just a temporary diversion from the big yellow banana. Small and light is important, so I can hoist it onto the Tempo's roof racks by myself. Of course, it would be nice if I could find something on sale that's set up for fishing.

That night on the Wholesale Sports web site, I immediately find the perfect match, a 10.5-foot "Angler," a molded sit-inside kayak specifically designed for fishing, with two rod holders and a trolling bracket on the front deck. It even comes equipped with an "anchor system," which the previous day I didn't think existed for a kayak. Best of all, it weighs only 48 pounds.

The next morning, I drive to the airport and transfer some items stored in the big yellow banana to the Tempo. Along with the kayak gear already in the trunk, I have everything I'll need for a brief test run in a new kayak. Then I head down Interstate-5 to Burlington. If I find the kayak I want, I plan to heft it onto the roof racks and head directly to the nearby Skagit River for my first outing.

The complicated simple life, originally confined to Canada, has migrated across the border.

◊ ◊ ◊ ◊ ◊ ◊

Chapter 7

Little Yellow Mango
Skagit River: Sedro-Woolley to Burlington WA

IN THE CAMPING SECTION OF THE STORE, several dozen kayaks are corralled together in two groups – tall and short. I head towards the short group, looking for a tan kayak, since the store's web site says it's the only available color for the Angler.

"Can I help you," says the young salesman.

"I'm looking for a ten-foot-six kayak called the Angler, but I don't see it here."

"Over there," he says, gesturing towards an orangeish-yellow kayak, suspended on a rack 6 feet above the floor.

"That's it," I say. "But it's supposed to be tan."

"Don't know about that," the young fellow replies. "I'll pull it down for you."

Once on the floor, I'm immediately sold. This is just what I need for the rivers around Bellingham.

"It's supposed to come with a troll mount on the front, according to your web site," I say, pointing to the place where I expect to see the mount but find only a plastic cap.

"Maybe this is it," says the salesman, popping open the cap. "Looks like an electrical connection, maybe for lights or something."

An electrical system on a kayak? I doubt it. Maybe this is the young salesman's first day in the kayak department.

When I inspect under the cap, I find a standard rod holder receptacle.

"Maybe the rod holder is stored somewhere," I suggest. "This is where it goes."

"It's an extra accessory, but you can buy one in the fishing department."

"I'm sure your web site says it comes with the kayak. It also lists an anchor system, but I'm not sure where it's attached."

"That's an extra, too," says the young fellow. "There's one over here for thirty bucks."

He reaches to a nearby shelf and hands me a box that seems overpriced for such a light anchor.

"Okay, I'll need that and the rod holder, but could you check with your boss to see if they're supposed to come with the kayak?"

"Wait a minute," he says. "Let's see what's in here?"

He unlatches the rear hatch, and reaches inside.

"They're both here," he reports. "Just saved yourself a bunch of money."

Yes, and I sold myself on this kayak without needing a salesman.

As soon as I verify the price, I hand over a credit card and my military ID as identification, avoiding my BC driver's license that sometimes confuses clerks.

"Wow! Are you in luck," says the salesman. "Thirty percent off plus another ten percent with your military ID."

So I sold the kayak to myself and got it at a forty percent discount. Not bad.

"Do you need paddles or a life vest?" asks the young fellow.

"I've got everything I need," I reply.

"How about a buoyant heaving line like this one?" he asks, handing me a red-bagged rope from the nearby shelf. "I think it's a legal requirement."

"Got one of those, too. I'm ready!"

"I guess you are. Do you want me to help you carry it to the parking lot?"

Actually, I don't need that either, if it really weighs only 48 pounds. But I accept his offer, although I insist on him leaving the kayak on the ground next to the Tempo.

"I want to load it up myself," I say. "I guess I should take the stickers off first."

The young salesman laughs, and then heads back to the store, with the kayak wedged between the Tempo and the pickup truck next to me. I pull off four stickers, insert the new rod holder into its mount, and lift the light kayak onto the roof racks. I attach two tie-down straps and connect the stabilizing ropes already attached to mounts near the Tempo's forward and rear license plates. It's a perfect fit.

The Skagit River is nearly in the store's back yard, so it's an easy drive to the Sedro-Woolley launch ramp Margy and I surveyed when we traveled with the big yellow banana. My plan is to make a short river trip today, just enough to test out the kayak and how to fish from it. Making this first trip in familiar territory should make my initial outing a lot more comfortable.

At the launch ramp, I phone Margy: "Can you pick me up at the Burlington launch ramp on the Skagit at 3 o'clock?" I ask.

"Sure. I guess this means you bought the kayak."

Angler kayak outside Wholesale Sports

"Yup. A half hour from purchase to the launch ramp at Sedro-Woolley. I'm ready to go!"

"How's the new kayak?" asks Margy.

"Small, if you know what I mean."

She knows, after living with the big yellow banana all these years.

"Just what you need," she replies.

I give Margy driving directions to the spot at Burlington, reminding her to have her cell phone handy in case I need to change the time or pullout location. From the Burlington ramp, she'll be able to quickly shuttle me back to Sedro-Woolley where the Tempo will be parked. Then I'll drive back to Burlington to get the kayak. Vehicle shuttles are a component of the complicated simple life of all river kayak adventures, even when you have an extra vehicle standing by.

At the Sedro-Woolley boat ramp, I find more activity than I've seen on the river. The salmon season is getting a lot of attention, and boats come and go at a rapid pace. I carry the empty kayak down the ramp and position it off to the side, trying not to interfere with the

Launch ramp at Sedro-Woolley

constant traffic up and down the ramp. Then I go back to the car for the rest of my gear, which I carry down on a second trip.

Two boys are fishing at the base of the ramp, reeling in small suckers nearly as fast as they get their lines in the water.

"You're probably having better luck than these guys with boats," I say to them.

The curly redhead grins: "Caught one about this long a few minutes ago," he says, spreading his hands about a foot apart.

"Better than they did, I bet," I say, gesturing to the boats bobbing offshore, waiting their turn to pull into the ramp.

I load the kayak, double-checking I have everything I need. My collapsible fishing pole is in the rod holder, rigged up with a trout lure that should work for salmon. I wade into the water, pushing the kayak in front of me. Then I get aboard as gracefully as I can in any kayak, and I'm on my way.

As I enter the river, I watch two boats ahead of me, anchored near a logjam, with another boat slightly farther downstream. The fishermen's poles are bent, indicating the significant pull of the current.

Tied-up boats fishing for salmon in Skagit River

Drifting past the boats, I immediately miss the luxury of the rudder on the big yellow banana. In this Angler, I can paddle on one side to steer, but that draws the vessel sideways, unless immediately corrected. I'll need to learn how to maneuver adroitly without a rudder, but it won't be a problem on this wide river today. For now, I'm being pushed downstream at a rate of about 4 miles per hour, seldom needing to paddle except to correct my heading.

My pullout point is only 5 miles ahead, as-the-crow flies, which means about double that distance on the meandering river. At this pace, I'll be there in a little over two hours, which includes some fishing along the way. All is perfect for my 3 o'clock meeting with Margy at the Burlington ramp.

My first landmark is the Sedro-Woolley Bridge. Maybe I can start fishing now, and troll right under the bridge. That's a bit bold, but fish are known to hang out under bridges, aren't they?

I fumble with my fishing pole, extending it to it's full length, and ready to try my first session of river drift fishing. Without considering

Sedro-Woolley Bridge

the physics of the situation, I decide to start right out by casting my line and beginning a troll-drift downstream.

I'm still not sure whether this is legal. I'm quite sure you can't fish while under power on the Skagit, but probably there's nothing wrong with drift fishing.

It doesn't take long for me to learn the error of my ways, whether legal or not. Just a few seconds after my lure hits the water, my line is extended nearly to its full length, pulled along with my kayak by the strong current. That doesn't allow any room to play a big fish, so I start to reel in a few feet of line. Almost immediately, I snag something underwater. Without any extra line to play with (and no way to paddle back upstream), the fishing line snaps, breaking right at the reel connection. So now I have no lure and almost no line left. My tackle box is full of lures, but no extra line. Within five minutes of entering the water for the first time with my new kayak, my day of fishing is done. Now I understand why drift-trolling in a river isn't a wise idea. And now I understand why local boats tie up to a snag. It's not just a matter of state laws – it's a matter of the laws of physics.

My fishing line and lure aren't all that's missing. When I reach into the watertight forward compartment for my camera, I notice my cell phone isn't there. If it isn't in this compartment, and not in my pockets, it must be in the aft compartment behind me, which is unreachable from my seat in the kayak. This will complicate things if I have to update my arrival time or pullout destination with Margy. Of course, I could go to shore to use my phone (assuming I didn't leave it back in the car). But it reminds me I need to get my act together for future trips. "Slow down, Wayne," I say to myself out loud.

There are more boats on the river than I'd expected, enjoying the third week of salmon season. In the next few miles, I pass numerous fishermen standing in their waders or on gravel bars. As I paddle past, they all seem to notice my fishing pole poised on its mount, since they all have the same question.

"Seen any fish?" they ask.

"No, but I really don't know what I'm doing."

They laugh. But they'd laugh harder if I explained I lost all of my fishing capability on my first cast.

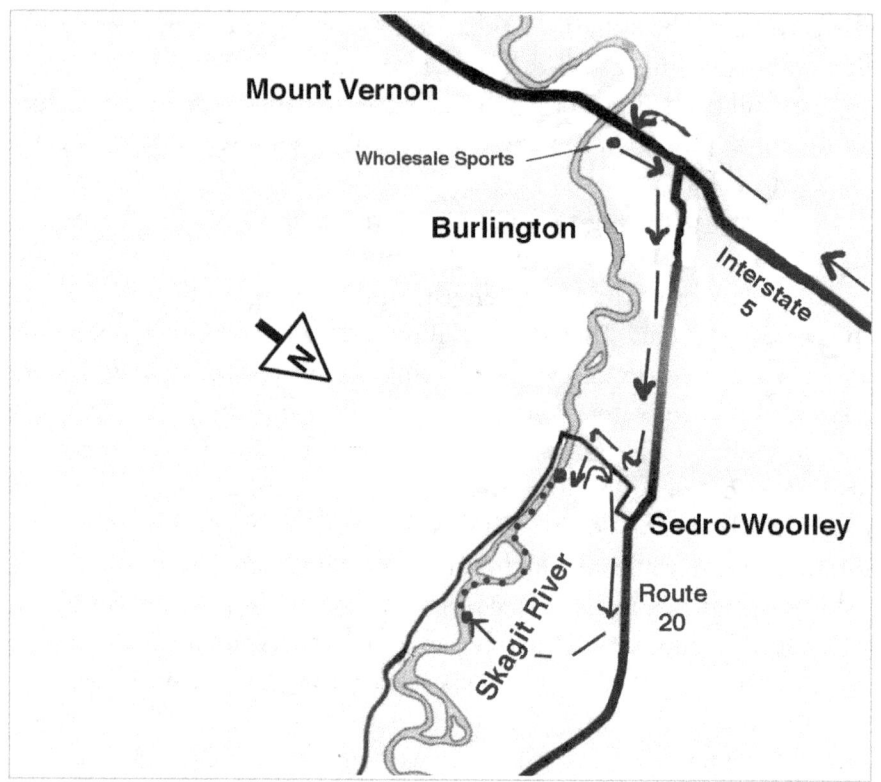

First river trip in Angler kayak

With today's fishing out of the way, I have plenty of time to experiment with paddling in the current. I try to maneuver quickly, as a test for rivers where fast turns will be necessary. Here in the Skagit, there's no need for immediate heading changes, so I don't pay much attention to my lack of rudder. What I don't discover yet is how easy it is to turn a rudderless kayak in a swift current with proper practice. Later (one trip too late), I learn the proper technique – simply put a paddle in the water for immediate drag to turn in the desired direction. It's too bad I don't learn this skill today, because I'll need it tomorrow.

Waterfowl are abundant this time of year, and I pass a group gathered in a small floating flock. I'm unable to specifically identify the species before they scurry off, but I get a picture for later examination.

Unidentified waterfowl on Skagit River

(Afterward, I'm still unable to identify the birds, although they seem similar to a large pintail duck.)

As I approach my pullout destination at the Burlington ramp, I maneuver around several powerboats as they come and go. On the high bank next to the ramp, a few fishermen have thrown their lines in the water. They've probably been fishing more than 5 minutes without losing their rigs.

Today has been a good test run for me, although I could have experimented more with rudderless maneuvering in the current. But for now, I'm able to steer adequately for a river like this. And I've learned how not to fish in a river from a kayak.

When Margy sees me paddling towards shore, she compares the kayak to the big yellow banana by dubbing it the "little yellow mango," a name that sticks. There's quite a contrast between our big sea kayak and this small vessel that fits so compactly on top of the Tempo. The little yellow mango will provide me with lots of thrills in the days ahead.

Arrival at Burlington launch ramp

Center-of-Book Photos
British Columbia Destinations

Getting around on Powell Lake, BC

Mr. Kayak on Powell Lake, BC

Telegraph Harbour, Gulf Islands, BCos

Margy in *Mr. Kayak* on Lois Lake, BC

Norway Island, Gulf Islands, BC

Mowat Bay, Powell Lake, BC

Sit-on-top kayak at floating cabin, Powell Lake BC

Mr. Kayak at Floating Cabin, Powell Lake, BC

Floating logs clog Horseshoe Lake, BC

Nanton Lake, BC

Chapter 8

Paddling Lesson
South Fork of Nooksack River WA

THE NEXT DAY, under threatening skies, I drive eastward on Highway 532. The forecast is for showery conditions, and the sky over the mountains ahead seems ready to meet that description. But the air is still warm for early October, and I wouldn't mind a few drops of rain. Certainly, it won't be significant enough to need the kayak spray skirt stored in the trunk.

Rather than continue up the North Fork towards the fishing spot where my Toyota gave me trouble, I follow the south spur of Highway 9, turning towards Acme where the road parallels the south (lower) fork of the Nooksack. At Potter Road near Van Zandt, I turn right towards the one-lane bridge where I plan to pull out of the river. Margy is scheduled to meet me here at 4 o'clock, then shuttle me upriver to my car, wherever it may be parked. I still haven't decided on my launch spot, but Potter Road looks like the ideal pullout location.

A turnoff just before the bridge is wide enough to accommodate several vehicles, although I'm the only one here now. The dirt road down to the water could probably be negotiated by the Tempo, but it will be easy to simply walk the 48-pound Angler up from the water after I pull it out of the river.

I drive back to Highway 9, turning right towards Acme. Farther up the road, I get several glimpses of the river as it runs through open fields and occasionally right next to the highway. At one spot, two cars are pulled off next to the river. If I don't find a launching place near Acme, I can return here to consider using this spot.

Crossing the bridge leading into Acme, the area near the span looks ideal for a launch – wide, with no whitewater visible. Beyond the bridge, on my left, is a well-kept parking area, complete with a freshly painted white fence. Four cars are already parked here, with clear trails leading over to the river. The town of Acme has put a lot of work into providing access to the Nooksack.

I chose the trail that leads upstream, walking the route without the kayak. And I walk and walk, realizing this is going to be a long haul, even with a light kayak. Additionally, a second trip will be necessary to haul the rest of my equipment. So before even reaching the river, I turn around and go back to the car.

The other path is shorter, heading downstream slightly, but it ends at a 5-foot cliff that descends to the water in a muddy drop. Climbing down, even without a kayak, would be challenging. Launching here isn't realistic. But from this perspective, the other side of the river near the bridge looks ideal. From there, two paths down through the bush seem evident, both ending on the same wide gravel bar.

I leave the car in the parking area, and walk back across the bridge to inspect the potential launch site. On the road running parallel on the other side, two turnouts are evident, but so is the threatening sign that clearly announces *No Parking* and a second warning *Vehicles Will be Towed*.

At the second turnout, I hike down the short path to the gravel bar. It's a path that will be easy to navigate with the little yellow mango. I can park briefly in the illegal turnout, quickly haul the kayak down to the river, and then move the car back to the white-fenced parking area on the other side of the bridge.

At first, my plan works well. I walk back to the parking area for the Tempo, and drive it across the bridge, parking in the turnout. It takes only a few minutes to offload the kayak and my equipment. Once everything is on the gravel bar, I think through what I'll need on this river trip. Cell phone – double-check after yesterday. I'm ready.

So I drive the Tempo back to the parking area, and walk (again) across the bridge. I move the kayak closer to the river, and begin loading my equipment.

Launch location above Acme Bridge

When I begin to zip up my life vest, I realize there's something missing. My GPS (normally clipped to my life vest) is back in the car. I used it on the roads today, and then promptly placed it under my driver's seat, as I normally do to keep it out of the sight of potential thieves. That's my excuse for missing it when I unloaded the car. But it's a piece of equipment that seems important on a river like this. I'm sure Lewis and Clark wouldn't launch without their GPS.

My mental checklist was good, but not quite perfect. So I take the time to walk back across the bridge (again) to retrieve the GPS, and then cross the bridge (again) to return to the kayak.

Looking down the river before launch, the pool under the bridge looks ideal for fishing. I probably shouldn't stop right after getting the kayak in the water, but I want to be ready as soon as a fishing opportunity arises. So I put my collapsible fishing pole in it's forward mount, and extend it in a ready-to-go position, with a sparkling pink-and-black lure attached to the line. Then I use my cell phone to call Margy, asking her to pick me up an hour later than originally proposed due to my delayed start. Finally, I'm ready to go.

Just as I'm about to push off from shore, a young couple with a golden retriever on a leash park in the *No Parking* zone, and walk out onto the gravel bar.

"Going fishing?" asks the man.

"Along the way. But mostly just paddling downstream to see the river. Is the fishing good here."

"You should be able to find some salmon. Do you have some Dick Nites?"

"Got 'em, but I might try some trout lures."

The fellow nods, while simultaneously giving me a look that implies this is Dick Nite country, and don't forget it.

"Do you think I'll have to walk my kayak through low water between here and Potter Road?" I ask.

"Might have to, but you should have pretty good water."

I step off from shore, straddling the little yellow mango, plopping down in the seat when the water is deep enough. Not a bad entry under the pressure of public observation.

I immediately face my first challenge. I've been studying the gravel bar that is at the limit of my vision, only a few hundred feet downstream from the bridge. To my eye, it looks like a dead end, but certainly that can't be true. After all, the river under the bridge is running strong, although fortunately without whitewater. It must go somewhere.

On my GPS, this obstacle shows as a big island, with almost equal widths of river on each side. As I get closer, I can see the right side of the island is completely dry, blocked by fallen trees and big rocks. No current flows in that direction. But now I can see an opening to the left, although only about 8 feet wide. So all of the water under the bridge must run through this narrow path. And I can hear it!

The dynamics of the situation confirms this will be quite a torrent, although I can only see the entrance where the river bends to the left and disappears out of sight behind the island. As far as I know, I'll be facing situations like this all afternoon, so I might as well just grin and bear it.

Of course, after the fact, I realize it would have been wise to go ashore on the wide gravel bar directly ahead to inspect the situation to the left before jumping in without looking. It would have been a

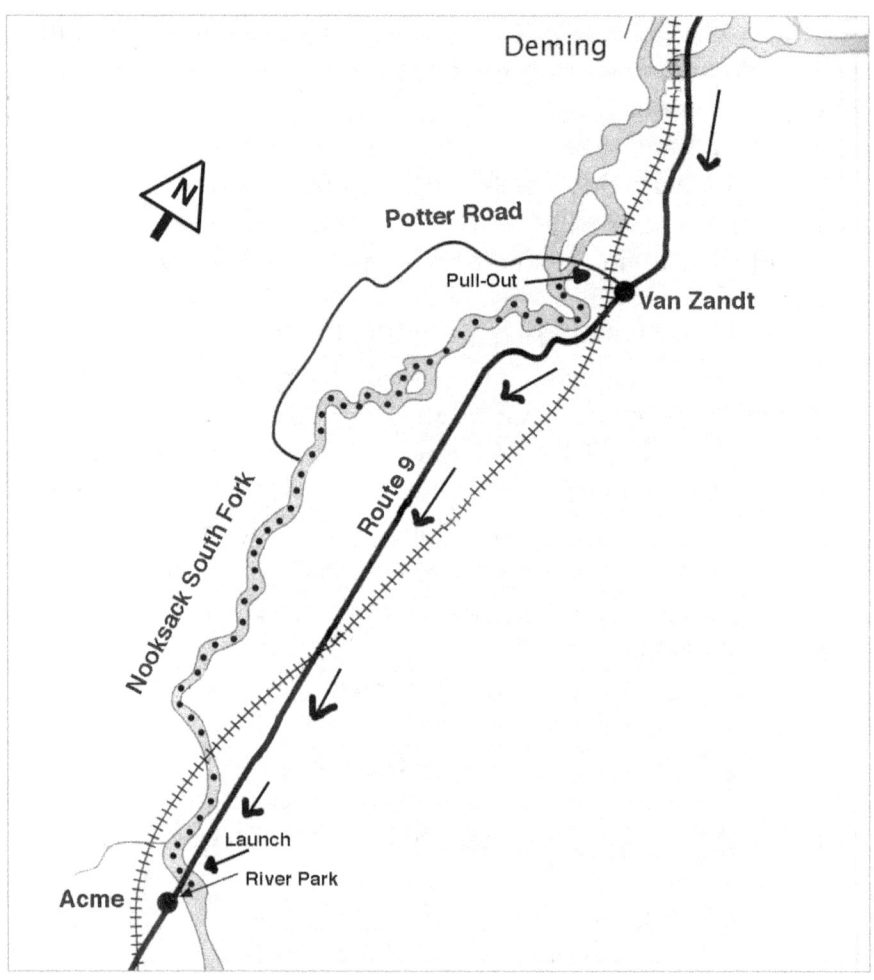

Nooksack South Fork – Acme to Van Zandt

simple solution, but I ignore it. Chalk another one up to my recent self-instructions to "Slow down."

As soon as I enter the flow, I have to paddle hard to avoid the branches that line the left side of the river. Beyond that obstacle is a nearly straight run that quickly picks up speed. It will be my first real chute as a kayaker, and I'm lucky it's so straight. On the other hand, I'm unlucky it ends in a logjam that spurts out into a deep pool.

The little yellow mango stays in alignment fairly well on the way down the chute, and I'm wise enough to simply dip a paddle in the direction I want to turn. This works well all the way down the almost-whitewater channel, but I change my strategy as I approach the logjam.

The jam consists of a single fallen tree centered in the narrow river, lying almost flat, roots towards me. I'm unable to tell whether the tree is perfectly straight or angled to the left or right, so I'm not sure which side of the split chute to select.

Approaching the logjam, with the narrow river even more restricted, tumbling whitewater pushes to both sides. I decide the route to the left looks better, maybe a little less turbulent, so I paddle hard on the right side of my kayak. Of course, a slight dip of my left paddle would have been wiser. Not only would it have been more efficient, it would have prevented the kayak from slipping sideways. But I haven't learned this lesson yet.

A few seconds later, already awkwardly sideways, I decide the right side is better. It seems wider, so I dig in with strong left strokes. The kayak corrects to the right, but I'm rapidly running out of time. And now I can see that the route to the right isn't a clear path either. A partially-submerged branch of the fallen tree juts out to the right, and I'm going to hit it!

My small kayak is now skewed to the right due to the hard paddling I've done on the left side. For a brief moment I think I might pass over the submerged branch, but it's too close to the surface. Wham! – I hit the branch, which shoves me up and to the right, and then I roll upside down in the water. It happens fast.

I'm out of the overturned kayak in a flash, still hanging onto my paddle, in water shallow enough that I can feel the bottom. I grab the upside-down kayak before it gets away, and drag it out of the swift current and towards the gravel bar now in front of me. A few feet from shore, I pull the yellow mango upright as I beach it. My water bottle promptly pops out and starts to float downstream. When I reach for it, I notice my cloth fishing kit floating downstream as well. I go after the kit, but somehow drop my paddle in the process, and it and the kayak begin to get away from me.

I grab the fishing kit with one hand and the kayak with the other. I sling the kit onto the shore, quickly pull the kayak out of the water, and literally toss the 48-pound mango (plus contents) onto the gravel bar. I wouldn't have guessed I possessed such strength, but funny things happen in demanding situations. Then I go after the paddle.

Within a few minutes, with paddle in hand, trudging my soaked body back to shore, everything settles down. I begin to laugh (at

Below logjam after the roll-over

myself). All is well – I'm unhurt, the kayak seems undamaged, and all of my equipment (including my paddle, minus one water bottle) is accounted for. Even my electronic GPS, cell phone, and camera are dry in their waterproof pouches. I'm not even cold (yet), although thoroughly drenched. The south fork of the Nooksack is the warmest section of the river.

As I take an inventory of items, I lay them on the rocks to dry. Then I notice my fishing pole, still pointed upward in the holder. It looks normally collapsed, but it isn't. The two-foot stub is all that's left of the extended pole. Riding briefly upside down in shallow water took its toll.

I laugh again. This trip began only a few minutes ago. And right away, I've overturned my kayak and broken my fishing pole. On the other hand, the sun is shinning bright, while dark clouds blanket the mountains to the east. I'm lucky to be able to dry my body and my equipment in the warm air. And when I check my fishing pole more closely, I find the reel still works, and I can still cast with the stubby rod. If I catch a salmon today, it will be quite a fight.

Shortened fishing pole

I relax and enjoy my time in the sun. Then I'm on my way again. Thinking through what has happened, I experiment with dipping paddles in sections of the river where the flow is rapid. It becomes obvious this is the technique to use in a swift current. It's unfortunate I learned this a few minutes too late.

The rest of the trip is anticlimactic, but thoroughly enjoyable. Birds of all types are abundant on the South Fork, including geese, eagles, and Stellar Jays darting across the river. I gain from my overturning incident, both in terms of paddling control and learning to take the kayak to shore in advance of precarious situations, to look over the run of the river ahead. Sometimes you just have to learn the hard way.

At one deep pool, I pull the yellow mango against a logjam to fish. I get one bite, but it's too small to be a salmon. Even a trout would be quite a catch on this shortened pole.

While I fish the swirling water with my stubby pole, my attention is called to thrashing in the water behind me, about a hundred feet upstream. At first I think it's a bear, since the splashing is so sizable. Then I consider that it might be dogs playing in the river, because

Fishing near logjam – South Fork of Nooksack River

there are several large splashes a few feet apart. But there are no dogs in the water, only splashing. Then the mystery is solved, and I realize I'm watching salmon. In a few more minutes, the thrashing in the water resumes at a spot even farther upstream.

Farther down the Nooksack, I reach an area where the flow widens and becomes so shallow that I run aground. I walk the kayak to deeper water in order to continue. At other shallow locations, I walk along the shore, steering yellow mango with its stern line through fast water full of obstructions.

I pass fishermen on the shore. Many of them are couples sitting in lawn chairs with their poles angled out into the water, enjoying a mostly sunny day on the river. Like me, they don't look like it's that important to catch any fish.

"Any luck?" yells one man from shore.

"No, but I haven't been trying very hard."

It's the truth.

Approaching the Potter Road Bridge pullout, at a final bend in the river near a gravel bar, a young couple in their chairs point at me while they talk between themselves.

"How am I doing?" I yell to them.

"Looks good from here," the man yells back.

"But you didn't see me when I flipped over back there."

He laughs, probably thinking that I'm kidding.

My learning curve is improving, maybe a little too late. But definitely not too soon.

Chapter 9

Water, Water, Everywhere
Skagit River: Hamilton to Lyman WA

My next river trip, from my launch spot north of Hamilton to the proposed pullout north of Lyman is a road distance of only two miles, and a winding river distance of merely 5 miles. But it will serve as another test of the kayak, with plenty of anticipated opportunities to practice my steering in swift current. Plus, I'm building in lots of time for fishing without being rushed. I even have a new fish pole for this trip, rigged with a Dick Nite lure and sinker on a y-swivel. For variety, my previously foreshortened pole will also stand ready with a spinning lure.

Back in Bellingham, I run my equipment checklist, which includes plenty of water. It's tempting to pack only the drinking water I'll need for this trip, but it's wise to include an additional jug just in case a short trip turns into an unexpected overnighter. Considering the clarity of the freshwater in the Skagit, readily available in an emergency, it's a bit of overkill, but a good habit. This jug's screw-on cap was a leaker on a previous trip, with a few drops of stray water in the aft compartment offering no harm. Still, I twist the plastic cap tight, just to be sure. In the hallway from the den, I pile the jug along with my other equipment, all ready to go.

A half-hour later, when I return to the hallway stack, everything is wet. The jug has fallen on its side, and water has poured all over my backpack, fishing kit, camera (fortunately sealed in a baggie), shoes, and author's notebook. The floor is wet, so I mop up the remaining water, and dry my equipment as much as I can. I'm not yet to the river, and things are already soaked.

I drive south on I-5, exiting near Burlington on Route 20. After passing Lyman, I turn off the highway on Hamilton Cemetery Road

(Cockerham Road), which winds through farmland to Lyman Ferry Road, where a ferry must have crossed the river a long time ago. I park at the wide turnout near the river. This will be the pullout spot I've described to my friend, Jeanne, so now I phone her to provide details for her scheduled meeting with me in another four hours.

"When you leave Route 20, it's quite a ways to the river. You come to a stop sign right away, then continue straight for a while, which turns into a road that winds through several farms. Just keep going until you see trees on your right that mark the bank of the river. Then turn onto Lyman Ferry Road, which is clearly marked."

"Sounds simple, so I'll try to keep it that way," she replies.

Maybe she's referring to her recent bout of getting severely lost when trying to meet Margy and me at the Conway Bridge.

"Once you get here, you should see a fisherman standing in the water on the other side of the river. He's there now."

"Don't you think he might be gone in another four hours?"

"Probably not. Guys around here are crazy about fishing."

Jeanne laughs, but I'm betting she finds someone fishing on the other side of the river when she arrives. I've been here several times, and it seems there's always a fisherman.

"I'm not sure there's cell coverage on this stretch of the river," I add. "But I'll call as soon as I come ashore with the kayak. My phone works here, so we shouldn't lose communication."

We didn't lose communication at Conway either, but it still took almost an hour for Jeanne to find me below the bridge. I decide not to mention it.

Before leaving the pullout spot, a big blunt-bowed aluminum boat pulls up onto the adjacent gravel bar, and a fisherman walks ashore. The river's water level currently prevents bringing a boat directly to shore, but I'll be able to walk the kayak to land through shallow water when I arrive.

While the fisherman waits for his support crew to arrive with a trailer for his boat, I ask him about the fishing.

"I'd rank the season as 'average,' through I got a few big ones today."

"Remind me," I say. "What's the status of the legal season for the various types of salmon?"

The fisherman goes through a complete list of salmon, which goes in one ear and out the other. I hear the fisherman tell me Silvers

(Chinooks) are open now, and he says something about Pinks, but I doubt I'd be able to tell one from the other if I had one on my hook. Fortunately, as a catch-and-release guy, I shouldn't get in trouble with the authorities.

From the Lyman Ferry pullout spot, I drive north through Hamilton, looking for a good place to launch. Originally, I planned to go farther up Route 20, beyond Rasar State Park. But I don't want to be faced with such a long paddle that I don't have time to fish. So when I find a good riverside spot just beyond Hamilton, I make a quick decision to launch from here.

As I offload the kayak from the Tempo, the wind begins to gust, and big maple leaves rustle around my feet. The sky has turned threatening quickly, although this mid-October day is supposed to remain partly sunny. Before all of my gear is loaded in the kayak, a few raindrops are already falling, and the breeze is whipping around rather significantly.

The wind is coming up the river, but certainly the current will win when it comes to any need to paddle. Still, I've never been on a river in gusty conditions, so I approach the launch process cautiously. I

Skagit River launch ramp above Hamilton

wait a few minutes, but nothing changes. Farther west, downriver, the sky is brighter, so maybe I should try to catch up with better weather. Upriver, it's a lot darker. I wonder how quickly a downpour upstream will affect the flow down here?

Paddling away from shore, the wind pushes me sideways. I easily recover, but have to work to stay pointed downstream. The wind opposes the current, and it slows my progress more than I expect. But within half a mile, all settles down, and I'm paddling in the sun. More noticeable than the loss of the wind or clouds is the sudden reduction in noise when the gusts disappear. Now I can hear the current flowing around a logjam ahead, and I get ready for my first steering challenge.

I try dipping my paddle to steer in the swift flow, and it works efficiently. This time I'll be ready.

This logjam and the others I encounter today are mostly easy to handle. And with only five miles to travel, I have time to spare. For the first time in this kayak, I'll be able to leisurely fish along the way, and I take advantage of the situation. At the first backwater pool, I tie up to a snag near the shore. Casting out into the nearby swift current, my yellowish-green Dick Nite rig drifts downstream into the quieter water. As the sinker drops deeper, I feel it bounce along the bottom, seeming like a perfect opportunity to catch a salmon. Once my lure stops in the deep pool, I let it rest there for a few minutes. Then I retrieve my line, and go through the process again. Best of all, I fish for at least fifteen minutes without losing a single lure. That's progress.

There's more water in the Skagit than I've seen before, and the river is wider. But the current seems slightly reduced overall, possibly because the increased width prevails over the volume of water. The water is as green as during the summer, but not quite as clear.

I don't catch any salmon today, but I enjoy fishing at several places where I tie-up to snags. At one spot, below a logjam, I fish long enough to notice several changes in the river's flow near shore. Water swirls in brief bursts – whitewater spurts over the rocks – and then runs silent for a few minutes, and again bursts like a surging spout. Somewhere upstream, something has changed, maybe a small logjam breaking lose and changing everything farther downstream. I watch the bursts of swift current repeat themselves through several cycles, and then I move on.

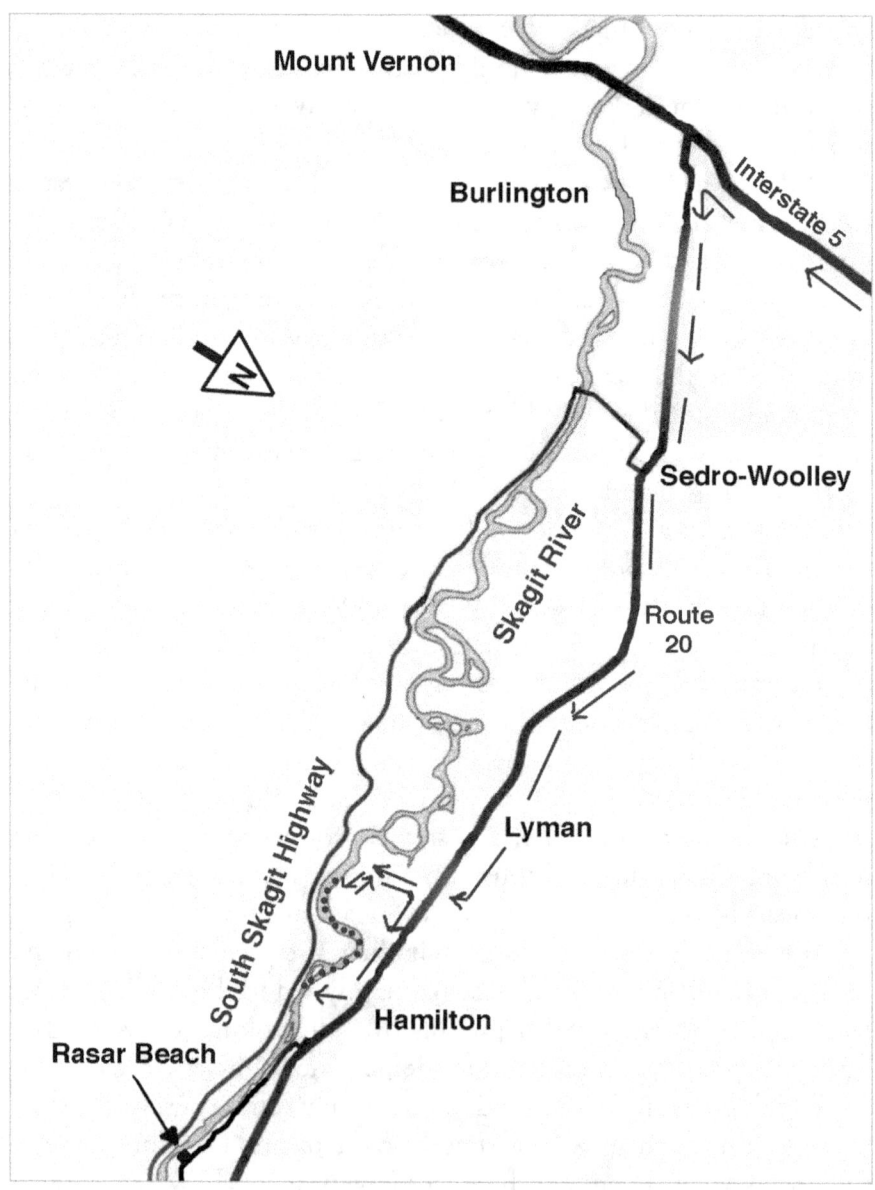

Hamilton to Upstream of Lyman

At one fishing spot, my luck at retrieving lures runs out. Tied to a logjam near shore, and fishing with my Dick Nite rig strung out downstream, I decide to cast a spinning lure with my shorter pole.

With the Dick Nite rig in the rod holder, I use the other pole to cast my spinning lure. With both lines in the water, and one hand awkwardly balancing my paddle, the spinning lure snags an underwater obstacle. When I try to retrieve my other line (the Dick Nite), it too becomes stuck on the bottom. Both lines are snagged at the same time.

The current is running fast a few hundred feet downstream. The sound of the extensive whitewater hasn't escaped my attention while I've been fishing in this spot, but now I plan to try to retrieve at least one of my rigs by releasing my rope to the logjam and drifting over one of the hooks. I doubt I'll be able to retrieve both lures before running out of space above the approaching whitewater. In fact, the current looks so strong that I plan to paddle all the way to the other side of the river (after dealing with my snagged hooks), where I'll go ashore and hand-line the kayak along the shallow side of the river.

My plan quickly falls apart. Once untied from the logjam, I drift rapidly downstream. I struggle with my paddle, while simultaneously holding the pole with the spinning lure, aiming for the area where it's snagged. I quickly pass over spot without retrieving my hook, and then grab the other pole from the rod holder. So I now have two poles and a paddle in my hands. I pull hard on the line with the spinning lure, and it breaks.

Setting the pole aside, I notice I'm already well past the spot where my Dick Nite rig is trapped. I pull hard on that pole now, breaking that line, too. Both rigs are gone, and I'm now so far downstream that I'm not sure I can avoid the turbulent flow on this side of the river.

(Okay, you can say it. I sure have a lot of fishing disasters. That's why I consider it a challenging "sport," or a better word might be "battle.")

I put the second pole down, and paddle hard, aiming for the far shore and slightly back upstream. Going against the current, there's no opportunity to merely dip a paddle to steer. Instead, it's a matter of power paddling with all of my energy.

I think I'm making some headway, but the out-of-control roar of the downstream water overshadows my progress. In fact, the water in that direction is moving back towards me in what looks like a sudden tidal surge!

I've never seen anything like this before. The water downstream seems to be moving rapidly upstream towards me. Now it's catching me!

How can this be? It's illogical to encounter such a situation, defying the laws of physics. Yet, whitewater is swirling towards me – rushing upstream!

Then I realize what's happening. While trying to cross the river, and attempting to paddle upstream, the current has become so swift that it has overtaken me. I'm now in the full thrust of the tumbling flow. It hasn't come upstream to find me. Instead, I've swung downstream so swiftly that I'm the victim of an optical illusion. Whether I planned it or not, I'm in the midst of the swift water I've attempted to avoid.

The good news is my kayak is treated like a log by the powerful current – taken on a ride through the swiftest flow, but it's the most direct path to the downstream end. I dip my paddle a few times to help control my course. Within a few more seconds, I'm out of trouble, spit out into a deep, quiet pool. In a very brief period of time, I've traversed this dangerous spot in the river, almost totally at the mercy of the elements. It happens so fast I don't have time to worry about what's going on.

The rest of the trip is uneventful, with another stop for fishing after rigging my collapsible pole with a replacement lure. Like my previous stops, I catch no fish, but this time I get some minor nibbles, and see a few salmon splashing in the water nearby. These big fish aren't interested in my hook, but at least I don't lose any more lures.

Clouds move overhead again, and a shower spurts on me in big drops. By the time I get to my pullout spot at Lyman Ferry Road, it's pouring hard. Fortunately, I'm wearing raingear that keeps me comfortable.

I walk the kayak over the shallow bar near shore, and then up onto the muddy beach. By the time I've removed my equipment from the kayak, I see Jeanne's car coming down Lyman Ferry Road towards me. I turn around to look across the river, hoping things are as I left them when I pulled into this spot with the car 4 hours ago. Sure enough, a fisherman is still standing in the river on the other side. These guys never give up.

◊ ◊ ◊ ◊ ◊ ◊

Chapter 10

No Shuttle Required
Silver Lake WA

River trips generally require a shuttle back to the launch point. In swift rivers like those of northern Washington, there's no alternative once you find yourself downstream. In contrast, most of my paddling has been on the coast of British Columbia, where it's easy to return to your launch point. No shuttle required.

Lakes provide a similar advantage of not requiring a shuttle. If you're without an extra set of wheels (and another driver), lakes and oceans have their advantage. One day when I'm faced with such a situation, I decide to find a location for a day of lake paddling. Since no one will need to retrieve me, I consider remote lakes far inland, as devoid of human activity as possible. On the map, Silver Lake, north of Maple Falls and almost at the Canadian border, looks perfect. Not only is the climb in elevation significant, suggesting remoteness, there's a public launch ramp at the adjacent state park.

On a sunny October day, I drive east on Highway 542, crossing the Nooksack, then through Maple Falls to the left turn at Silver Lake Road. It seems appropriate that the maple leaves are turning yellow and orange in Maple Falls. Silver Lake Road is a pleasant uphill climb, meandering through farmland and horse country.

The state park is nearly devoid of visitors this day, leaving the well-groomed picnic areas and campsites quiet, and the launch ramp parking area empty. I'm pleased to find a newly constructed dock adjacent to the concrete ramp. Although the shore is wide open, providing an easy launch spot without a ramp, I'll be able to use the ramp and dock, not even getting my feet wet.

Launch ramp at Silver Lake, Washington

A sign cautions: *Swimmer's Itch – Swim at Own Risk*. Launching without wet feet sounds even more appealing now. And I'll fit in well with a notice that also warns: *No boat motors over 10 horsepower*.

When I put the kayak in the water at the base of the dock, a harmless-looking green scum floats the shore, extending out twenty feet into the lake. Could this be an indication of an area of swimmer's itch? Just to be more safe than sorry, I slide the kayak over to the dock without stepping into the water, tie up to a cleat, and load my gear from there.

Getting into the small single-person kayak, an unstable operation under any circumstances, is more precarious from the dock's higher platform. With my fishing pole already in it's forward rod holder and angled over the dock (a mistake), I lower myself into the vessel with a quick shift of my weight off the dock and downward. Making sure my aim is perfect, I hit the seat solidly, without upsetting the little yellow mango. But the jolt and rebound on the rope connecting me to the dock jams my fishing pole back under the dock. Fortunately, fish rods are designed to bend a lot before they break.

Now the fishing pole can only be relieved of its stress by either pulling myself back up onto the dock (initially bending the rod farther) or trying to slide away from the wooden structure gently, without breaking the pole. But I still have a line tied to the cleat (another mistake), which is now stretched to its limit, causing the kayak to tip decidedly upward on that side. The result is a paddler aboard a cockeyed kayak, connected rigidly to a dock by a taut line, with a fishing pole wedged at a near-breaking angle. Leave it to me to make departures interesting.

I struggle with the docking line, finally easing the now-overly-tight knot loose. The kayak slips away from the dock (except for the fish rod's increasingly-bent connection). I push off the wooden structure slowly but firmly with my paddle. The tip of the rod slides free and swings all the way down to the water with a quick splash and an immediate rebound. My expected "easy launch" is finally behind me, and I'm bobbing without further problems, clear of the dock. Live and learn.

As I paddle out into the bay, the water remains shallow over a thick weedy bottom. In fact, even after considerable paddling, I can still see green-covered rocks. I've checked the fishing regulations for this lake, which indicates standard rules for all species, but what kind of fish should I expect to find. Originally, I would have guessed trout, but this bottom looks more appropriate for bass.

Before leaving the south end of the lake, I try a few casts using a red-and-white daredevil, my favorite lure for fish of all kinds. On nearly every throw, I catch weeds right away, but it's easy to break the lure loose from the bottom.

Even under these conditions, I experience several bites that are obviously small fish. Paddling out towards the middle of the bay, the water is still only a few feet deep. I float here for another half-hour, casting and pulling off weeds.

Even before I leave the bay, so far to the south it wraps out of sight of the main lake to the north, I can see this is a different landscape than I expected. The mountain lake charm is wonderful, but houses line the shore as far as I can see. Widely separated, the dwellings at first seem like permanent residences, each with its own boat dock. But then I notice most of the docks are empty, an almost-sure sign no one is home. At one location, there's a big pontoon boat with a tiny outboard motor, and a chainsaw is operating invisibly near the house. At another, a large boat of more traditional design (again with a small motor) marks the spot where a wood chipper is grinding up logs near shore. The house at this spot is three full stories, much grander than my perception of traditional lakeside cabins occupied on a part-time basis. But this is what I conclude dots the entire shore – seasonal cabins, many palatial in scope, but most vacant in October.

I paddle past a big lodge on the boundary of the state. I look into the spacious dining room, with chairs stacked upside down on the tables. There may be guests here, but there's no evidence of them inside or on the grounds surrounding the building. As for the lodge itself, repair work is underway on the piling below the shoreside of the building, with a trail of yellow tape marking the "keep out" border separating the construction from the large dock (which is empty).

All of this off-season activity is creating quite a racket – hammering below the lodge, the chipper's *snap-zoom, snap-zoom*, and the noise of the chainsaw. So much for a peaceful high-mountain lake in October.

The water deepens as I paddle north, but I can feel bottom when I cast with my lure, only a few seconds after it hits the water, even in spots far from shore. Most retrievals result in weeds on my hook. By now I'm nearly convinced this isn't a trout lake. I'd love to catch a fish to find out what's here, but I don't get another bite.

On the northwest shore, I find a more permanent small village where about twenty homes line the lakefront. Most of the docks here are occupied with what seems to be the vessels of choice – boats 20 to 30 feet in length with puny outboards that look funny on the back of these big boats.

Crossing over to the east shore, I pause to nibble on a chocolate-coated granola bar and sip on a plastic straw stuck into a small box of orange juice, one of my favorite on-the-water snacks. Before resuming my paddling, I pull out my camera from its watertight bag and take a picture. To the north, I'm looking at Canada only a few miles away.

Here in the middle of the lake, I can cast my line and paddle-troll in what must be the deepest part of the lake. I successfully avoid the weeds and don't encounter any snags. Neither do I find any fish.

After returning to the southern end near the state park, I try fishing once again in the shallow water where s wooden footbridge marks

Silver Lake, looking north towards Canada

the "Fishing Point" I've seen designated on signs along the shore. This elaborate multilevel structure would be ideal for an afternoon when dad wants to introduce his young son or daughter to fishing, with lots of cubbyhole platforms to stand on and drop a line.

The water is only a foot deep here, with a preponderance of thick weeds. I struggle with my casting, constantly hanging up on the bottom, but I'm always able to recover my lure. When my red-and-white gets caught on the bottom, it's easy to position myself over the lure and whack it loose with my paddle. For an environment filled with weeds, I don't lose a single lure the entire day.

Passing under the elevated portion of the bridge, I paddle into a small lily-pad-covered bay that seems ideal for fish, although probably not trout. On several casts, I experience a bite, and finally reel a small fish all the way to the side of the kayak. I don't want to harm this fish, so I reach into my fishing bag to find a pair of pliers to extract the hook before hauling the 10-incher out of the water. While I'm floundering for the pliers, the fish jumps off my hook and is gone before I can get a close look. During the brief period when the fish is near the boat, I notice a nearly pure silver coloration and thin body. The color seems wrong, but the shape right for a trout. Maybe the silver shading is how these waters were named – Silver Lake.

Paddling back to the dock, I reflect on the fact that the lake has been totally empty of operating boats, except for my kayak. Imagine how busy this place must be in the summer when boats of all sizes (with tiny outboard motors) zoom everywhere. With the 10-horsepower limitation, water sports must be limited to cruising, fishing, and towing kids on tubes – no water skiing.

When I get back to my launch point, I decide to pull into the concrete ramp and get my feet wet rather than fighting the dock again. It takes only a few minutes to get the kayak unloaded and hoisted onto the Tempo. Just in case, I take off my water shoes, wipe my feet, and put on dry socks without further delay, wanting to avoid "swimmer's itch."

By the time I begin snugging up the straps on the rooftop carrier, two fishermen pull into the area, towing a 14-foot aluminum boat behind their small camper. As they prepare to launch their boat (with a small motor boasting a "9.9" decal on the front case), one of the men asks the obvious question: "Catch anything?"

"Some bites. Even got one almost into the boat before I lost it."

"Lots of fish in here," he replies, which gives me the chance I've been waiting for.

"What kind of fish do you catch here? Looks like bass water to me."

"Rainbow trout, and lots of them. Some cutthroats, too. But you have to fish in the deeper water near the middle of the lake."

The fishermen are efficient at launching their boat, and they soon motor out of sight. Alone again on the shore, I sit in the Tempo's driver's seat, my legs draped out the open door. The long shadows of late afternoon provide a colorful contrast of water, land, and sky, so common this time of day near lakes in the backcountry.

Two plovers flitter from the grass near the shore into the water right in front of me. They splash around, enjoying a bath. It's their own personal excursion to the shallow water of a small lake at the end of their day, no shuttle required.

◊ ◊ ◊ ◊ ◊ ◊

Chapter 11

Saltwater or Fresh?
Dakota Creek WA

WHEN I'M LOOKING FOR A PADDLING LAUNCH SPOT that won't require a vehicle shuttle, the ocean shore or a river delta is a good choice. If you properly time the tides, you can get a good ride upstream towards freshwater, then back down to your launch point when the tide changes.

Dakota Creek just south of Blaine, Washington, seems a likely location, so I research the fishing regulations on the Internet to determine the limitations and any special regs. Rather than muddle through a thick regulations booklet, I've become accustomed to searching the listings online with a key word. "Dakota" provides an immediate hit, and just the one I'm looking for – Dakota Creek is still open to fishing in early November, with the added restriction of single hooks only.

Since I've been losing a lot of lures in a variety of rivers lately, my stock of single hooks is down to three Dick Nites. But these lures are for stationary fishing in swift current (particularly famous in the Skagit River). I don't expect a rapid flow in Dakota Creek. Besides, I'd prefer to cast in deep pools, drifting slowly and enjoying the scenery. I find several large red hooks in my tackle box that are not mounted on lures, and I remember they came with the treble-hooked lures I purchased. There's obviously a way to swap the hooks, but I can't figure it out. Maybe there's a spring mechanism inside the lure that allows a quick disconnect. I work at it for quite a while, and finally give up, without finding an obvious way to swap the hooks. I could use some more heavy lures anyway (best for distant casting), so I'll detour to the sporting goods store on my way to Dakota Creek, and purchase a few single-hook lures.

Most of the appealing Blue Fox lures I prefer for casting sit at the end of the store's shelf, arranged from heavy to light, top to bottom. The heaviest lures seem too big for today's outing, particularly since I have no idea what kind of fish to expect, so I settle for the next smaller size. But the lures with the best colors (to me) have only treble hooks, so I shuffle down the counter to another brand of lures. Nothing seems to suit my fancy, but I continue to browse, nearly talking myself into purchasing some of the less-appealing ones.

Meanwhile, a store supervisor arrives in the Blue Fox area, restocking the shelves. Maybe this will result in some single-hook lures of the weight I desire.

"Can I help you?" he says, as I glance down the aisle.

"Well, since you asked..."

I walk over to the Blue Fox area, and hesitantly ask my question: "You know, I can't figure out how to swap out hooks. Some of mine came with a treble hook attached, but with a single hook in the package. I've tried to swap them, but I must be missing something."

"No, there isn't a special trick," he says. "You have to cut off the old hook and crimp a new one on. Not easy."

"That makes me feel better. I figured there had to be a simpler way, but I sure couldn't find it."

"This is a good one," he says, handing me a lightweight fluorescent green Blue Fox with a treble hook. "They've been catching a lot of chinooks on these lately."

"Thanks," I reply, looking the small lure over, and then returning it to the shelf. "But I need something bigger, with a single hook."

The salesman runs his finger along the two rows of bigger lures, and stops at the perfect specimen I've been looking for all along – a single-hooked bright orange Blue Fox. How did I miss it, or did he just restock it? I leave with two orange lures and an additional dull green lure that would have been my second choice, if I'd seen it earlier.

In the parking lot next to the sporting goods store, I take the time to rig up my fishing poles. On my full-size casting rod, I hook on an orange Blue Fox. The green lure goes on my new collapsible pole (which replaces my rod damaged by the overturned kayak). How could any fish resist these beautiful displays?

Then again, who's to say there are any fish in Dakota Creek? On the other hand, does it really matter? To me, the joy of paddling and fishing is more than adequate repayment for my efforts. For hours, I once fished a high-mountain lake that looked full of trout, without a single bite. Later, when I learned this lake was sterile, it didn't bother me a bit. The experience is vastly more important to me than the catch. It's a good thing that's true, because my fishing record is horrible.

* * * * *

ON THE DRIVE UP INTERSTATE-5 towards the Canadian border, my mind shifts to the prospects of today's paddling and fishing adventure. I can't begin fishing at my launch spot, since that will be saltwater, and I have only a fresh-water license. So I'll have to wait until I enter the creek. But wait a minute – where will my freshwater-only fishing license take effect? The fishing regulations booklet should specify the details, but I don't have one handy. I hadn't noticed any specific location for the change from fresh to saltwater when searching the Internet site. In fact, is Dakota Creek even considered freshwater? After all, the kayak guide indicates you can ride the rising tide nearly all the way to the creek's origin, at which point it dissipates into a narrow trickle. So maybe the entire creek is considered saltwater, and I don't have a license to fish it. When using my online search word ("Dakota") I skipped right to the correct page, but I didn't notice whether it was in the saltwater section. In other words, I'm out for a day of paddling and fishing, and I don't even know if I'm legal. (Later, checking the hard-copy edition of the regulations, I find Dakota Creek in the freshwater section, with legal fishing beginning as soon as I leave the mouth at Drayton Harbor.)

Today's first look at Dakota Creek is provided when I cross the bridge, driving north on I-5. It's plenty full, but not rushing like the Nooksack this time of year.

Leaving the interstate, I cross the creek again at the Blaine Road Bridge, stopping on both sides to seek a launch spot. The banks are high and covered with thick bushes, with no spot adequate for launching a kayak. There are access points both upstream and downstream from here, but it's all private property.

Turning right at Drayton Harbor Road, I spot a dirt road to the right just before crossing California Creek, and then another unoccupied turnout on the other side of the bridge. I use the turnout to return to the dirt road, where two cars are parked just off the paved area. There's room for a third, so I pull the Tempo into the muddy spot.

This is the northeast shore of Drayton Harbor, and a wide gravel bar sits only a few hundred feet away, below the 5-foot cliff that leads to the water at this location. But there's no way to get to this perfect launch spot without hauling my kayak down the cliff, then weaving along the rocky shore to the gravel bar. Instead, I elect to launch right below the parking area, against the rocks.

Fortunately, my kayak weighs only 48 pounds, so I'm able to heft it down the vertical incline by perching it on the top of the cliff, bow pointed towards the water, then reaching up and sliding it off the cliff. I

Launch site at Drayton Harbor

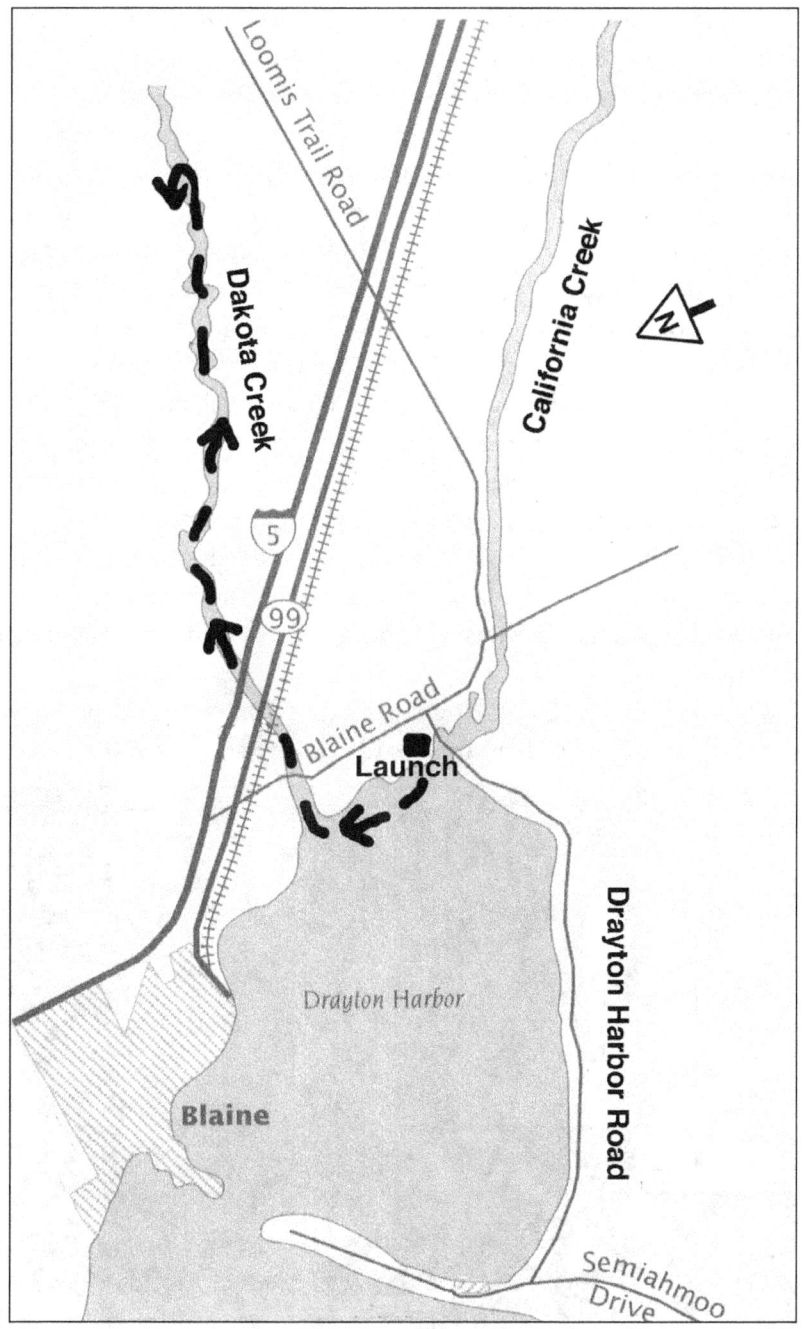

Dakota Creek and Drayton Harbor

find a secure spot for the vessel on the narrow shore that's approaching high tide while I return to the car to gather up the rest of my gear.

Back at the Tempo, I pack up the few items I'll need for this day trip. But as I sit in the car, preparing to don my water shoes, my sense of organization quickly deteriorates. I can't find my GPS life vest clip, and one of my water shoes is missing. For a moment, I consider wearing my regular shoes, which wouldn't be a major problem on this short trip. I can probably get into the kayak without getting my feet wet, and I don't plan on stopping anywhere along the way. So I should be able to keep my feet dry until I return to this launch spot.

At the last minute, I find the missing shoe, sitting right where I put it – on the car's dashboard, crammed down where it's out of sight. Not a typical place to leave a shoe, of course. This car has everything I need for kayaking, if I can just find it. I rig a temporary clip for my GPS, which should work okay for today. When I don my life vest, I find the original GPS clip already attached to it. I swap over to the better clip, and laugh at myself, which is one of my favorite sources of humor.

With no further delay, I push off from the cliff, and paddle out along the gravel bar. A fisherman wades in the shallow water near the

City of Blaine from Drayton Harbor

bar, casting out as far as he can, so I give him wide berth by navigating farther offshore. From here, I can see around the promontory, with the city of Blaine perched on its majestic wide cliff. Just around the point from here, big homes line the shore.

High tide is scheduled for two hours from now, which will help push me up the creek. Then, after slack water, I'll turn around and use a tidal assist downstream, arriving back at the car well before low tide. Drayton Harbor can drain nearly dry on the northeast shore, making getting back to the California Creek Bridge difficult without deviating way out into the bay. But now, as is always the case near high tide, it's hard to imagine water leaving this large basin so quickly.

Approaching the bridge on Blaine Road that marks the official mouth of the creek, I taste-test the water by dipping a finger – very salty. I'll continue this taste procedure all the way up Dakota Creek, but never do I find freshwater. Even at my maximum upstream location, the water is saline.

Under the bridge, I pause and let the kayak drift. The breeze is from the east, pushing me back towards the harbor even in this flooding tide. The tidal flow is inland, but the wind wins. Still, this is better than paddling into a wind with an opposing current.

Blaine Road Bridge

The area immediately upstream from the bridge looks like a perfect fishing pool, but I defer to the fact this is definitely saltwater, and I respect that my license is probably not valid. And there's lots of civilization surrounding me (each homeowner obviously ready to report anyone fishing in the wrong flavor of water), so I decide to keep my fishing line dry for now.

Right around the bend, four parallel bridges span the creek. The first is an active railroad, then Peace Portal Road (I-99), and finally the I-5 twin-span.

Below the second bridge, two men and a woman are fishing from the big rocks that mark the northern pilings, casting and retrieving their lines as I pass. I wave, they all wave back simultaneously, and I yell to them: "Is this considered freshwater, as far as fishing licenses are concerned?"

The woman and the man next to her ignore me. The other man waves his arm sideways while simultaneously scrunching his face, seeming to say he doesn't know or really doesn't care. Then again, maybe none of them have licenses anyway. What, me worry?

Approaching Interstate 5 on Dakota Creek

Passing under the I-5 twin-span, I mentally compare this bridge with the noisy (and scary) structure on the Skagit where the river passes under Interstate-5 near Burlington. Maybe it seems dramatically quieter here because it's a less-traveled section of the highway, or maybe the twin-span helps. In any case, it's no different than passing under any other small bridge today.

Beyond the interstate highway, the creek settles down to a less-urban waterway. There are still homes along the banks, but they're farther apart and less palatial in design. This is a different creek, narrower and more remote, with high banks on both sides. Great blue herons nest in this area in large quantities, generally found as solo encounters where a huge bird goes airborne with giant strokes of its wings, swooping low along the creek, to settle again just out of sight.

Canada geese, gulls, and ducks are also plentiful. And probably fish, but my good-looking Blue Fox lures raise nothing all day. But the best news regarding fishing today is I don't lose a single lure.

Like giant snowflakes, autumn leaves drop from the trees along the banks, and at some quiet pools, leaves form a layer that covers the

Mid-section of Dakota Creek

surface like interlaced lily pads. In most sections of the upper river, the upstream tidal flow is evident, but the breeze is still in opposition, and ruffles much of the surface.

The stream narrows even more, and shallow whitewater ripples become more extensive near gravel bars. I paddle a few hundred feet farther upstream, and stop near a minor logjam in a deep pool to snack on crackers and juice. There's no breeze in this protected area, but a check of my watch shows the tide has already turned. The narrowing creek contributes its now noticeable downhill flow to the reversed tidal conditions.

Upper section of Dakota Creek

I drift slowly downstream, leisurely paddling, and achieving a nice forward speed. There's something about autumn on the water that always feels special, whether it be a lake, a river or the ocean. Fall is a time for reflection at a more unhurried pace. I paddle back to the harbor lazily, on a near-perfect November day.

◊ ◊ ◊ ◊ ◊ ◊ ◊

Chapter 12

City Lakes
Lake Samish, Bellingham WA

WHEN BOTH TIME AND SHUTTLE TRANSPORTATION ARE FACTORS, nearby lakes are a wise solution. Most cities have a lake nearby that you can paddle, maybe even inside the municipal limits. Of course, the big disadvantage is the population density you're generally trying to escape during paddling adventures. On the other hand, when you're on the water, an envelope of solitude can surround you, even in the busiest settings.

On a sunny November day, with both time and vehicle shuttles limiting my choices, I drive down I-5 to Lake Samish. This is a cute little lake I always pass on my travels south from Bellingham, just out of town and easily visible from the highway.

The launch spot I've located on an Internet satellite photo is near the far end of the lake, accessed by Lake Samish Drive, which parallels I-5. So I continue past the first Lake Samish exit to the South Lake Samish turnoff at Nullen Road, reverse course immediately and travel northward along the shore. Big estates are prominent on this lake, and all of them block public access. But the public launch ramp is clearly marked, where Lake Samish Drive angles closest to Interstate-5. I pull off the paved surface into a wide area with a concrete launch ramp and plenty of parking.

A jungle of signs spells out all the rules, including *Vehicle Use Permit Required*. If you're a Washington resident, it's worth obtaining a fishing license just to get the coveted parking permit that provides legal parking access at many excellent kayak launch spots around the state. Some locals buy a fishing (or hunting) license just to gain access to great spots to walk their dogs. Although not all launch areas are marked *Vehicle Use Permit Required*, a surprising number carry this designation. Recently, at a remote, muddy single-lane access spot on the North Fork of the Stillaguamish River, I encountered one of these signs at a site maintained by the local fly fishing club. Parking fines are probably not common in such areas, but its nice to park where you know you won't be ticketed, and I'm pleased that part of my fishing license fee goes towards recreational access.

This well-maintained launch location on Lake Samish has plenty of other signs, plus a rack of "take one" handouts regarding lake regulations. I unload the kayak by the web of notices, and get ready to paddle. In this large public area, I'm the only person present, although several boat trailers are parked off to the side.

Lake Samish is open to fishing all year round, which is one of the factors in my selection today. It seems that a lake so close to the city, and with such a dense population of shoreline homes, won't provide the fishing opportunities I expect farther from town. Then again, I

Lake Samish launch site

haven't caught any big fish yet this year in the best-looking remote spots. The added benefit of being able to paddle and cast in wide-open stretches is particularly appealing to me.

Once I'm in the water, I push off far enough to evaluate which way I'll paddle. To the south, homes line the immediate shoreline, but the other direction is uninhabited for nearly a mile. So the choice is evident, and I paddle north along the shore.

This lake is deeper than I expect, with relatively high cliffs lining this side. It's a very trout-like setting where a mix of rocks, mud, and weeds form the bottom. (Of course, when I found nearly the same conditions in Silver Lake, I erroneously concluded it was bass territory.) I paddle only a few hundred feet, and then stop and begin casting.

Towering cumulus clouds line the north shore, and I'm already sweating, even with little paddling. I unzip my jacket, but I can't take it off, since it's under my life vest. So I go through the process of removing my life vest, and then my jacket; then I put my vest back on.

East shore of Lake Samish

It's a simple process on shore, but not so easy in the confined cockpit of a kayak. Still, it's nice to be stripped down to my T-shirt on a sunny November day.

In this relatively unpopulated section of the shore, the lake feels like a mountain escape, except for the constant rumble of nearby Interstate-5. The noise is loud enough that it's definitely annoying, and it must have a negative impact on the residents on this side of the lake. I glance across to the west shore, wondering if they too can hear the constant highway drone. When I lived in Los Angeles, only slightly farther from a major Interstate than this, it was quieter than in this reverberating hilly terrain. And wouldn't it have an effect on the fish? If I were a trout, I wouldn't consider these constant vibrations a desired habitat.

I head across the lake. On the way to the other side, trolling as I paddle, I make a wide turn before reaching the shore. Then I parallel the line of big homes nestled along the water. The noise from the highway is significantly reduced here, but it's still an obvious hum that annoys me, if only from the standpoint that it's so difficult these days to escape the imposition of bustling America.

This lake would be relatively easy to circumnavigate on an afternoon, but I'll leave that to more energetic kayakers. Instead, I'm content to paddle a little while trolling, stop and cast for a while, and then paddle some more.

As I cross back over towards the launch ramp, I stop mid-lake to snack on cookies and bottled water. Winding in my trolling line, I drop my lure directly below the kayak while I'm stationary, judging the depth as about 100 feet. I reel in just enough line to keep my hook off the bottom and let it bob in the occasional wake from the few boats that are on the lake with me today.

An expert water skier works his way back and forth along the west shore, trailing behind a high-pitched outboard motor. The boat stays a respectful distance from my small craft, but it disrupts my attempt to enjoy my surroundings. It's not the wake, which is minor, or even the nearness of humanity. Instead, it's the small addition of the outboard motor's hum to the drone of I-5. I'm glad I'm here, enjoying a warm autumn day on a pretty lake, but I'll take a quiet, remote location any day.

After resting mid-lake for several minutes, my fishing lure has found bottom while I wasn't paying attention. When I begin to reel in, I encounter a birds-nest in my slack line that takes a while to untangle. Just when I think the last kink has been eliminated, another knot develops. I finally end up breaking the line and retying it about 100-foot from the lure. It won't interfere with my casting, though it will now probably hang up as the reel unwinds during trolling.

While I finish up winding in my line, two boats launch from the ramp where I started. The first is a big metal fishing vessel that pushes out past me, plowing water. The second boat is still at the ramp, floating near shore while its occupants move their trailer into a parking spot. By the time I get back to the ramp, they're in the boat, still arranging their fishing tackle. Now that I'm close, I can see this is a serious recreational fishing boat, with tall chairs in a wide-open design. A small outboard sits at the stern, and an electric trolling motor is mounted on the bow. It reminds me of the bass boats seen on TV on Sunday morning fishing shows.

"How's fishing?" asks one of the men.

"No good for me, but I really don't know what I'm doing. Just enjoying it."

(By now, you must have heard this theme enough, with more hope for your own fishing adventures. Surely, no one has worse fishing luck than me. It's a good thing my enjoyment of majestic settings reigns supreme.)

Both men smile at my remarks, impressing me as fellows who understand. They came here late in the afternoon, probably directly from their daytime jobs, ready to enjoy a few hours on the lake.

"By the looks of your boat," I say, "there must be fish in this lake."

The older of the two fishermen grins at the compliment, and then replies in a determinedly slow statement of fact.

"Even a bad day on the water is better than a good day at work."

Oh, so true.

I pull my kayak out of the water and begin to load my equipment into the trunk of the car. When I return to the ramp to retrieve my kayak, the two fishermen have maneuvered out and along the shore, now fishing near the dock at the home adjacent to the launch ramp.

They cast and retrieve their lines like men who are enjoying themselves, just to be on the water on this beautiful day.

Fishermen on Lake Samish

Chapter 13

Up the Creek
California Creek WA

My original series of Canadian books in the series *Coastal British Columbia Stories* began with *Up the Lake*, and expanded to include additional titles that generally followed the "Up the" theme. Not surprisingly, I'm often asked when I'm going to write *Up the Creek*. There's nothing in my personal Canadian environment that indicates such a future title, but at least it's time for a chapter with this name.

California Creek is a minor waterway by State of Washington standards. Compared to nearby Dakota Creek, which could have been designated a river, I paddled California Creek with expectations for a much smaller volume of flow. On the map, it's clearly a shorter stretch from its origin, following Loomis Trail only a few miles to the creek's outlet at the bridge adjacent to Drayton Harbor.

On a mostly cloudy late November day, shortly after a major Bellingham snow storm (i.e., two inches accumulation, significant for this area), temperatures rise above freezing for the first time in four days. I've been waiting for conditions favoring a short paddle, although I don't expect much from California Creek. There's no fishing here after October 31, which means I'll not have the normal excuse for a paddle-and-pause trip that includes leisurely stops along the way. But my kayak guide indicates this short trip should provide a good bird watching opportunity this time of the year.

I drive north on Interstate-5, passing occasional patches of crusty snow along the highway that haven't yet melted. My wipers are necessary to keep the windshield clean, but the rain is light, and the forecast promises improving conditions in the afternoon, with temperatures in the low forties. At the last exit (274) before crossing the border into Canada, I pull off the interstate, drive across Dakota Creek at the Blaine Road Bridge, and look down on water that's noticeably higher than my previous paddle upstream. The local tide table shows it's now less than an hour past high tide, and the drop in water level will be gradual for the next few hours. Although this means I'll be paddling against the tide for my trip up California Creek, I don't expect it to be a significant obstacle, and the return downstream should be with a nice push. With these short late-November days, selecting a tidal condition perfect for paddling is little more than luck. Today, I've been relatively fortunate.

On Drayton Harbor Road, I cross the bridge and park immediately on the right in a turnout that can hold several vehicles right next to the water. Today, I'm the only occupant.

It takes only a few minutes to offload my small kayak and dress for the weather. Over my short winter coat and thick pants, I don a rain jacket and waterproof pants. Since the slow retreating tide is nearly at its high point, I'm able to launch in deep water right at the edge of the

Drayton Harbor launch site near California Creek

gravel parking area, allowing me to step into the kayak without getting my water shoes wet. This time of year, it's nice to start with dry feet.

However, when it's time to go aboard, it's actually more awkward than stepping into a kayak when it's grounded in shallow water. In theory, you only need to step into the hull with one foot followed quickly by the other, but it's easier said than done in a narrow bobbing craft.

I test the first foot, and then draw it back when the kayak dips to the side. After several awkward tries, I just go for it, trying to get my second foot aboard as soon as I can, while keeping my center of gravity as low as possible in an uneasy squat. For a brief moment, it feels like I'm going over, which would be the end of today's trip. Paddling in soaked clothes on a cold day would be unacceptable. But after a quick bob right and back left, I plop unceremoniously into the seat before the kayak tips over. Ouch! – but dry.

Once away from shore, I paddle around the edge of Drayton Harbor for a while, watching two small flocks of Canada geese takeoff with a display of splashing and honking, possibly disturbed by the sight of my kayak (a big yellow floating bird). The water is motionless in what looks like exact high tide, although the turn occurred over an hour ago.

Paddling under the bridge into California Creek, I see the first evidence of tidal current, with swirling water pouring around the large cement pillars. Clearance between the underside of the bridge and the water at high tide is less than six feet, so I paddle underneath feeling a bit claustrophobic, almost needing to duck my head to clear the structure.

On the other side, I'm greeted by a large expanse of calm water that forms a big slough. Birds are taking off and landing in nearly all directions. A great blue heron swoops low and slow past me, headed upstream. The bird's broad side exposed to me is marked by downy-looking soft blue velvet. Who needs to find an excuse to stop paddling today, even though fishing season is closed? The glimpses of waterfowl on today's trip are simply spectacular.

Paddling up the creek, I leave the broad "pond" behind, and begin to wind through an area of houses flanking both sides of the waterway. Except when I pull off into some of the dead-end bays along the way, I'm never out of sight of at least one home.

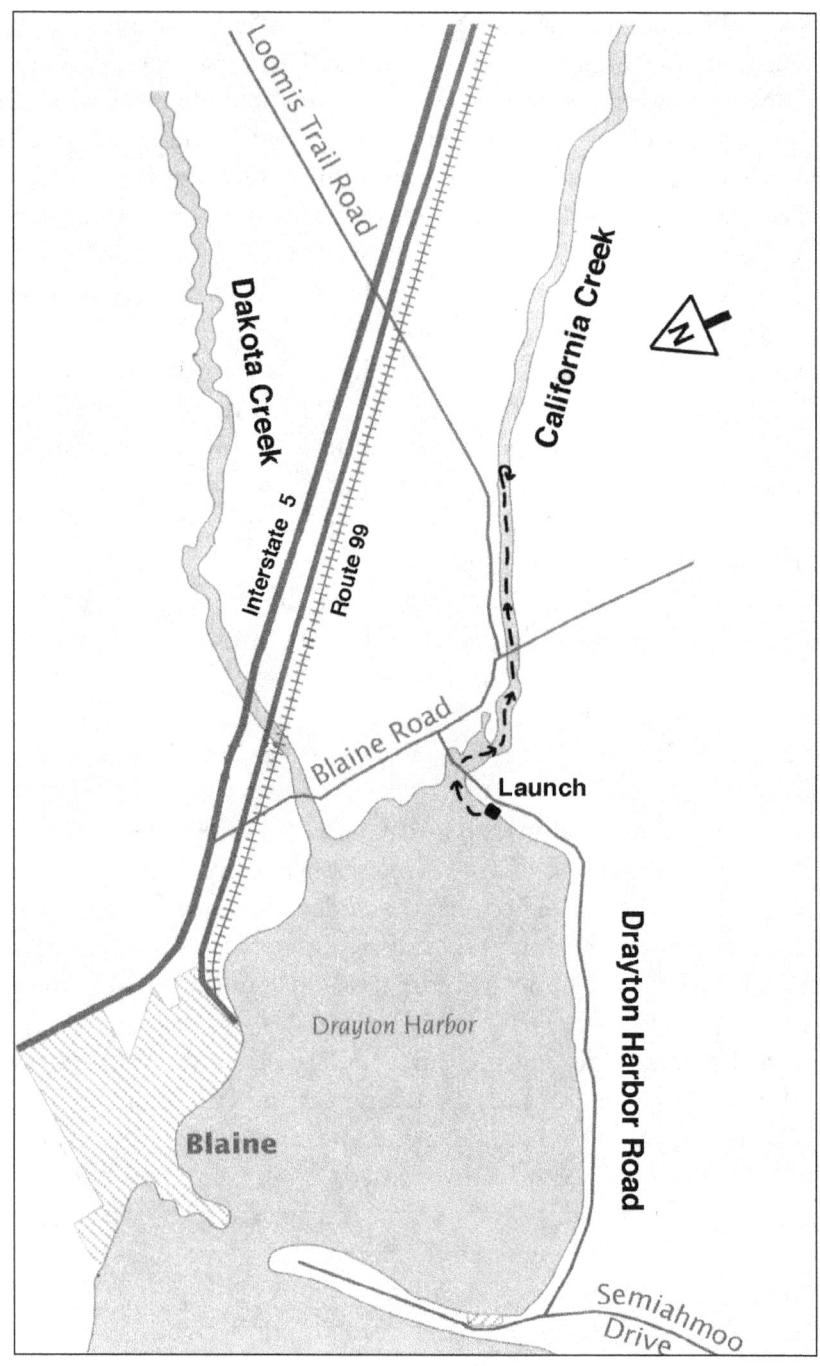

Drayton Harbor to California Creek

This creek is broader than I expected. Generally, it's straighter and deeper than I surmised, and full of pockets of foam that I initially link to the high tide. Then, when I approach closer to one of the bigger frothy ovals, I realize it isn't foam at all. It's ice!

At first, I'm not convinced it's really ice, so I swing my paddle onto the white floating swath, and the Kevlar tip rebounds with a high-pitched twang. It's ice, that's for sure, and lots of it. Besides the small floating sheets, I encounter some larger expanses measuring up to twenty feet long and nearly as wide.

How can this be? Sure, it has been cold the last few days, and there are pockets of old snow along the creek's bank in spots, but this is saltwater that's well above freezing temperature. I dip my hand into the water, and find it to be colder than I expected. But ice?

Not icebergs, of course – just flat sheet-like ice about a half-inch thick in most spots – but still a big surprise. Did this ice break off from shore farther up the creek and flow down to the mouth? One thing for sure, its an extensive feature on this creek today.

Seagulls form part of the bird population on the lower reaches of California Creek. Big gulls are perched on wood pilings near the

Ice sheets on California Creek

shore or bobbing in the water, generally solo inhabitants who come and go at a regular pace. I float past these birds without disturbing them. Unlike the Canada geese below the bridge, they act like I'm just another big yellow bird passing by.

Low bridges span the upper reaches of California Creek, jutting off from Loomis Trail, which parallels the stream. These are concrete structures, low to the water. Now, at nearly high tide, I barely clear my head underneath.

Just beyond the first bridge in this area, I paddle past a small cemetery that juts out as a narrow peninsula. It's well maintained, with colorful flowers marking many of the freshly-painted white crosses and glossy gravestones. But the cemetery is only ten feet above the creek. In fact, I'm barely looking up at the grave markers as I glide by. Spooky-looking from the nearby water.

The low elevation of the graveyard, coupled with the low concrete bridges, indicates this creek must never flood, though I'm not sure why it doesn't. This is rainy territory, and flash flooding would seem typical here. But apparently the creek stays within the banks I see today.

Bridge over California Creek

I don't paddle far. It's not that kind of an afternoon. Instead, it's a day meant for leisurely strokes and lots of pauses to watch the birds. I go far enough upstream to find a secluded bay that narrows as I continue into it. I'm out of sight of civilization here, and I stop when I reach a tree that has fallen across the narrowing flow. Massive ice sheets have moved into this area, and I allow my kayak to whack into them, pushing them out of the way when they're small, and navigating around them when they're too large to budge.

This is a different kind of waterway this time of the year, and a place I'm glad I didn't overlook because it seemed less challenging. There's something beautiful everywhere, and today proves that obvious fact.

Ice sheets on upper California Creek

Chapter 14

Willamette River
Corvallis to Albany OR

WITH MY U.S. KAYAKING LIMITED, so far, to northwestern Washington, I finally venture south in a giant leap. Several potential trips as far south as Seattle remain in my paddling plans, but there's an even bigger river trip farther away in Oregon – the Willamette River.

Since I travel to northern Oregon several times a year for college sporting events, it seems logical to try the Willamette. The river runs north from Eugene (where I often visit the University of Oregon), slowing its flow through Corvallis (home of Oregon State University), and then passing through Albany and Salem on its meandering route to join the giant Columbia River at Portland. My plan is to start somewhere between Eugene and Corvallis, where I expect to find strong currents that remain within my paddling abilities.

During an early February trip south, a winter break in the weather brings partly sunny skies and mild temperatures to Bellingham and the promise of several days of only occasional showers in northern Oregon. Temperatures are forecast to reach daytime highs in the mid to upper 40's. Such conditions are the best that can be expected in the Pacific Northwest this time of year. So Margy and I load up the big yellow banana on top of the Tempo. It will be a long, somewhat slow trip to Corvallis on I-5, with our speed restricted to the kayak's singing rope limit of 60 miles per hour – at least seven hours with a stop for gas and a quick meal.

After loading the big yellow banana at the airport hangar, I park the Tempo in the outside lot at our Bellingham condo, a sight that stops those who walk by. As I again explain to those who see *Mr.*

Parked and almost ready to go in Bellingham

Kayak on the Tempo for the first time: "It's really not a big kayak; just a very small car." In reality, it's both.

The trip down I-5 goes well, driving below the typical 60 mph rope-singing speed. Near sunset, we exit the main highway to cross Oregon's Willamette River at Albany, and then travel along Route 20 on the other side of the river for the remaining 10 miles to Corvallis. To our left, we're treated to several views of the Willamette, which flows at a respectable speed as we parallel its course upstream. From shore, a river always looks more daunting, and I sense Margy's apprehension. Yet this is the slower portion of the river, downstream (north) of Corvallis. My goal is the faster stretch on the upstream (south) side of Corvallis. I plan to launch near Peoria and haul the kayak out at Michael's Landing near downtown Corvallis, where we'll be able to find a taxi to take us back to our launch spot.

Dusk transitions to darkness as we drive the stretch of Route 20 between Albany and Corvallis. The Tempo's weaker-than-you-can-imagine headlights serve more as a warning to on-coming vehicles than a means to brighten the highway. The road eases away from the river, and then converges with it again as we approach Corvallis.

Darkness comes fast this time of year. We arrive at our hotel near Oregon State University, and park under a streetlight, which acts like a spotlight for *Mr. Kayak*. Maybe it's the wrong kind of security lighting for a college town where kids may enjoy discovering unique things on car roofs.

The evening's basketball game is thrilling (unless you're an Oregon State fan), with the USC women's team trouncing the Beavers in a never-in-doubt battle on the court.

* * * * *

THE NEXT MORNING DAWNS with the sun riding behind a high, thin overcast, with a forecast for an almost unheard-of winter daytime high of 54 degrees. We drive downtown to Peak Sports, which houses their two main recreational departments in separate stores – everything you could ever need for biking and paddling on adjacent corners. In the paddling store, a young female clerk is eager to provide advice, but she has a conservative slant to her counsel. When I explain that our river trip is planned to either begin or end in Corvallis, she's quick to recommend the easier route – downstream to Albany.

"I haven't heard much lately about conditions upstream," she reports. "It's generally a more challenging route. Some rapids to deal with."

That does it right there. Once Margy hears the term "rapids," they'll be nothing I can do to influence her. So I quickly give in, and inquire about what to expect on the downstream route to Albany.

"No problem along that stretch," says the clerk. "Some spots where there'll be strong current, but you'll be able to see it well before you get there. And the river is wide enough this time of year to allow you to navigate to deeper areas where the water runs slower. Should take you only two or three hours to get to Albany, depending on how often you stop."

"And whether we paddle much," I add. "I'm pretty lazy, you know."

She laughs, and then suggests that the swifter water from Peoria to Corvallis should also be within our limits. But it's too late. The word "rapids" has already taken its toll.

"Probably not up to that," I suggest to Margy. "At least that's what I'd guess."

"No," replies Margy definitively. "The trip downstream to Albany sound fine to me."

And so it is. We're headed north to Albany, with several prospective haul-out spots near enough to downtown to provide taxicab support. I'd prefer the pullout beyond the Albany bridges for a slightly longer trip, but we can evaluate it better when we get there. We'll have a cell phone to coordinate a taxi, and the trip back to Corvallis is only 10 miles.

"We really appreciate the free advice," I note to the young clerk. "Maybe we can buy a book or something to make it more worth your while."

"Over there," she says, pointing to a bookcase on the far wall. "Some good maps in some of them, if you don't have one."

We already have a guidebook for this part of the river, but there's an even-more-detailed map guide that will be handy on the river. And it also covers the river upstream, which should serve our needs for future visits to the Willamette.

From the sporting goods shop, we drive two blocks to the river, where a paved road along the water gives way to a dirt path leading us to the launch spot at Michael's Landing. With no one using the ramp at the moment, we drive right down near the water and park on the sloped ground next to the river. From here, we'll offload the kayak and our equipment, and then drive the Tempo back to the adjacent parking area.

The river is running substantially here, but obviously slower than we found on the Skagit during August. To Margy, this must look relatively inviting compared to some of the spots we've launched from elsewhere. She seems unruffled and ready to go.

As is often the case in nice launch locations like this, the spot doesn't stay vacant for very long. Just as we're lifting the kayak off the car, a fisherman pulls up and parks next to us. In a few minutes, he's out of his vehicle and casting out from shore with his long pole, and Margy strikes up a conversation.

"What kind of fish this time of year?" she asks.

"Just practicing my casts," he says. "No hook, just a dead weight. So are you headed down to Albany?"

Willamette River launch site at Corvallis, OR

"Yup," replies Margy. "Do you think the water will be this slow farther downstream?"

"Oh, it just gets easier all the way. I canoe this river to the south, where it's a lot more exciting."

"Looks plenty exciting to me, right here," says Margy.

"Shouldn't be a problem," he replies. "You can generally expect a headwind on the river between here and Albany, probably not much more than a light breeze today."

"Thanks," replies Margy. "And good luck with your fishing."

"Good trip," he says, while simultaneously returning to his casting practice.

While we finish up offloading our gear from the car, ducks swim back and forth on both sides of the river. Two mallards with dark green heads and white necks swim right next to our edge of the shore, paddling furiously against the current. Then they suddenly stop, turn around, and drift rapidly downstream, as if they're on a ride at Disneyland. What fun they seem to be having!

Fisherman practices casting at Michael's Landing

Today we'll encounter numerous birds – geese, ducks, herons, kingfishers. Many will float nearby, while others will stir up a ruckus as they takeoff and land on distant sections of the river. At our launch spot, more ducks walk along the shore, pecking for specks of food.

When all of our gear is out of the car, Margy moves the Tempo to the parking area. While she's gone, I notice something is missing from the pile of equipment next to me – our life vests. I'm sure the vests are not in the car, since I made a last-minute scan of both the back seat and trunk before Margy drove away. Of all the things to leave behind in Bellingham, nothing could be worse (except maybe paddles). Here we are, sitting on the edge of the river, ready to go, and no life vests.

How will I explain this to Margy? There are only two possibilities – we go back to the kayak shop (it's already approaching noon, with daylight slipping away) and buy two life vests when we have two perfectly good ones sitting in the hangar at Bellingham, or we paddle to Albany without them. Neither possibility seems pleasant, and I know one of the options Margy simply won't accept, nor should I.

Ducks at Michael's Landing, Willamette River

"Bad news," I say to Margy when she returns to the ramp.

"What?" she asks, knowing I'm trying to break the news to her gently.

"What would you say to paddling to Albany without life vests?"

"No way," she immediately answers. "What's wrong with those?"

She points to our two life vests, partially hidden on the other side of the kayak. When you're missing an important piece of boating gear, it might be wise to try looking on the other side of the boat.

"Thanks goodness," I say. "I thought we left them back at the hangar."

"Sorry," she replies. "I put them over there as soon as we started offloading stuff from the Tempo."

I'm not sorry. I'm overjoyed.

* * * * *

WE LAUNCH FROM MICHAEL'S LANDING without even getting our feet wet. Margy steps off the shore first, standing briefly in the partially grounded kayak. She sits down as fast as possible, before losing her balance. Then I go aboard the same way. When we're both settled in our cockpits, we push off with our paddles. There's a bit of scraping under the hull, but nothing alarming, and we're soon floating in deeper water, although drifting sideways. We struggle to get the bow pointed straight downstream, but then we're firmly in control.

"Rudder's down!" I report proudly.

With Michael's Landing barely behind us, two female rowers in an Oregon State University two-person crew boat speed past on the other side of the river, headed downstream at an impressive speed. Since they're oriented facing backwards in their small boat, they both wear caps with rear view mirrors to see what lies ahead. Their path is straight and swift. I wonder how far they're going, since they will obviously have to row against the current to get home. Then again, that's probably an important part of their exercise regime.

Within a few minutes, we're squared away in our cockpits, rudder down, and drifting nicely without paddling. I check the GPS for our speed – a steady 3 miles per hours. At this rate, we'll make it to Albany (8.6 miles as the crow flies, about double that distance on a meandering river like this) in less than 4 hours with minimal paddling. I expect the river to slow down as we progress, but we should never completely lose its pushing power, and there's not the slightest breeze to deter us. I remember what the fisherman practicing his casts back at Michael's Landing said: it's a rarity to paddle down this river without a head wind from the north.

Big herons, both blue and gray, swoop from shore to shore just north of Corvallis. Sometimes they sit on shore, relaxed enough to allow us to pass close without taking flight. As we pass near a blue heron, Margy snaps a photo.

We pass a power line near shore, where we come upon an osprey nest, a giant tangle of twigs on a pedestal purposely built for the birds on top of a power pole. The huge nest is one of many we'll see today atop these poles, where the electric company has decided to give these giant birds plenty of opportunities to use the poles without disrupting the flow of electricity. Ospreys insist on finding high supports (or denuded trees) for their nests, where they are far removed from natural enemies that might chose to attack them from below.

Blue Heron on Willamette River

On one older power pole farther downstream, where no pedestal exists, ospreys take over the entire top horizontal beam of the structure, obviously a less acceptable solution for both bird and electric company. Although we see a half dozen osprey nests today, none of them seem occupied with birds. Nor do we see any ospreys flying near the river.

Heron nests are also evident along the river, many of them built in bare-branched trees along the shore. Typically these nests are grouped into communities of five to ten nests, also vacant during today's winter trip downstream. But the herons themselves are easily visible flying to and fro along the Willamette on their huge wings, looking like long-necked flying reptiles of an ancient epoch.

A few miles downstream from Corvallis, we encounter the two women in the OSU boat, now resting in mid-river, taking a snack break. As we pass, one of the women yells over to us: "Going to Albany?"

"Yes. Is the river easy all the way," I yell back. "We're kind of wimpy, you know."

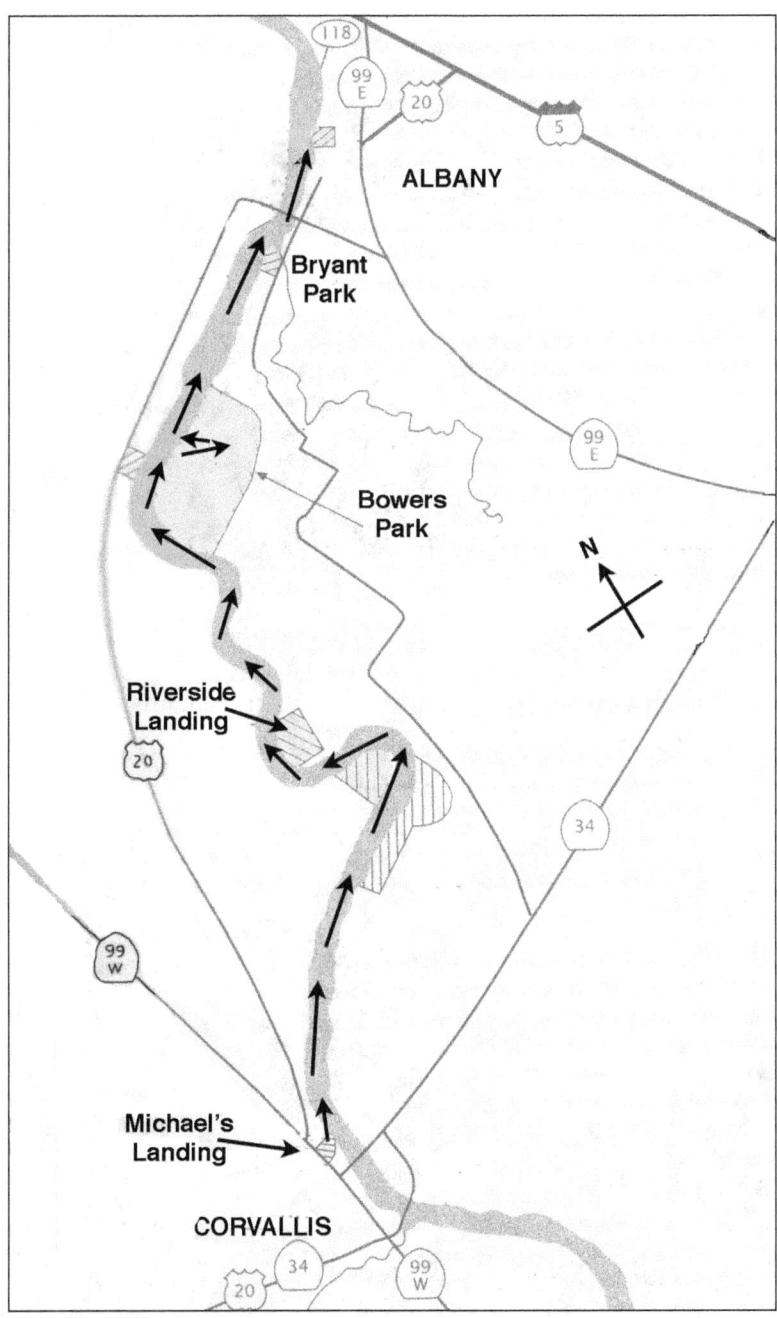

Willamette River from Corvallis to Albany, OR

Osprey nest on Willamette River

"It's fine all the way," she laughs. "You're from Canada?" she asks, obviously noticing the flag flying above our stern.

"That's us!" Margy yells back, not expounding further.

Heron nests on Willamette River

After we're well past the OSU women, Margy turns to me and says softly: "It's hard to explain. They probably think we're paddling all the way home."

"Which makes those buff college women seem kind of wimpy by comparison," I reply.

* * * * *

APPROACHING ALBANY, but with the twin bridges still around the next bend, we pass Hyak Park on our left. At first, the launch ramp isn't visible, even though the clerk at Peak Sports told us this is a popular launch and recovery spot for kayaks. So far today, except for the two college rowers, we haven't seen anyone on the river, and the Hyak ramp area is deserted. As we get closer, I finally spot the elaborate ramp, with a clear paved route to the river and cement stairs leading up to a fenced viewing area and picnic grounds. We glide past without stopping.

Almost immediately on our right is the entrance to the back bay at Bower Rock State Park, an undeveloped recreation area with a winding slough at the north end. We pull into the narrow channel and start inland, with the bay getting narrower as we progress.

Back bay at Bower Rock State Park

In these muddy waters, aquatic plants push nearly to the surface, a tranquil spot for our only stop of the day. We bob in the quiet at the end of the backwater, pulling out our juice packets and crackers with peanut butter. We're almost to Albany now, which should appear as soon as we exit the slough and swing around the bend.

Back on the main river, the flow is substantially reduced. The Willamette still pushes us, but only a few remnants of miniscule white wavelets are visible. The bridges of Albany now appear off our bow.

Of three possible pullout spots on our map, Bryant Park is first. The area is on our right before the twin bridges, and it looks acceptable but not ideal. Although it is a relatively flat beach, there's no evidence of an adjacent parking lot. Thus, it would be quite a distance to carry our kayak and equipment. So we continue on.

Next, on our left is Takena Landing under the twin bridges. This is a nice launch ramp, but it's on the wrong side of the river for easy access to the city of Albany. In front of us, a third bridge (a railroad trestle) marks the downtown area, with Bowman Park farther downstream on

Approaching the bridges at Albany

the right. It's now our intended landing spot, although it's farther from the trestle than I expected. We keep paddling, and soon a large dock is visible on the right bank, sticking out significantly into the river. I work the rudders, aiming directly for the dock, but then I realize the current is swifter than I thought. As we close on the wooden structure, it's obviously coming up too fast. I use full left rudder, swerving a bit too late. We make hard contact with our bow, but then rebound, and the kayak straightens itself as we're again pushed up against the dock by the flow. Perfect parallel parking, with no credit to the driver.

I crawl clumsily out of the boat onto the wooden deck without getting my feet wet, which means the whole trip was a dry-footed affair, a pleasant surprise. After my awkward exit, I hold the kayak against the dock, so it's a steady platform as Margy climbs out.

A few minutes later, Margy dials the number she's programmed into her phone for the local taxicab, but the conversation doesn't go well.

"No, we're at Bryant Park," she says. "That's on the Albany side of the river."

When she finally hangs up, I ask her what's wrong.

"I think the cab is from Corvallis, and he doesn't know Albany very well. But I think he's on his way now."

Meanwhile, a young couple and a little boy are exploring near the dock, stepping out tentatively on big logs half-floating near shore. They hear Margy's conversation, and offer their help.

"Are you trying to get a ride to Corvallis?" the man asks. "We'd be glad to drive you there. Maybe you could pay the cost of the gas."

It sounds good to me, and friendlier than a cab coming all the way from Corvallis. Margy phones the taxi again, and cancels our request for transport.

"The taxi was still trying to figure out where we are," she tells me. "So this ride should work out good for us."

I secure the kayak to the dock, in preparation for our trip back to Corvallis. Meanwhile a teenage boy approaches the dock, walking downstream along the river.

"Canadians!" he yells, as he gets closer. He knows his flags.

It's a leisurely and personal ride back to Corvallis to pick up the

Docked on Willamette River at Albany, OR

Tempo. By the time we return to Albany, load the kayak on the car, and start back to Corvallis (again), it's almost the same time as yesterday when we drove along the Willamette, southbound on Route 20. Same time, same road, same almost-worthless headlights.

Margy drives cautiously along the winding road. I notice she glances to her left at the river paralleling our course. This time, she looks a lot more relaxed.

Chapter 15

Go North, Young Man
Fraser River BC

IT WASN'T ONLY THE DEATH OF NEIL ARMSTRONG, but that certainly was an influence. On my sixty-sixth birthday, while thoroughly enjoying myself at my floating cabin on Powell Lake, I heard about Armstrong's death on CBC Radio's evening news. The headlines had a big impact.

I had just finished (back-to-back) Don Starkell's kayak memoir travelogues, *Paddle to the Amazon* and *Paddle to the Arctic*. As the Canadian summer was coming to its end, I realized that I hadn't tackled a single overnight camping venture all year, to say nothing of a lengthy kayak voyage. Reading Don Starkell's books awakened the need-to-paddle, but it seemed too late this year.

Turning 66 wasn't a particularly memorable occasion, until I heard the news about Neil Armstrong. Although I felt extremely healthy, I knew I could get "old" at any moment, particularly if I allowed myself to dwell on the concept. So I refused to think about it... except a little bit.

Next summer I'd tackle a major paddling adventure, without letting another year slip away. I discuss this with Margy, suggesting we consider another "pusher" river, like our trip down the Skagit or Willamette. *Mr. Kayak* and the old Ford Tempo were currently in Canada, and would remain there over the winter, so a Canadian destination seemed logical, but I had previously concluded (without significant research) there was nowhere in nearby British Columbia that would meet the criteria of a "pusher" that didn't push us beyond our whitewater rafting limits (which are minimal in a sea kayak).

"How about the Fraser?" asked Margy.

"Hadn't thought of that," I replied. "The Fraser has a reputation for being mighty swift, but there must be an area where it transitions from the whitewater of the mountains to the slow tidal flow of Vancouver."

We had traveled across the border into the States to find the gentle pusher criteria we wanted. But why had we gone so far when there were places like Hope and Chilliwack?

So I began to research the lower Fraser River, and realized I was missing out on a hidden gem in sea kayak river adventures. I had ignored the Fraser, although a river trip from Hope to Fort Langley seemed to meet our criteria just fine.

Maybe it wasn't too late to do a trip on the Fraser this year. Labor Day weekend was only a week away, and Margy and I had planned to travel to Bellingham with her mom (and cat) in the big Buick called "Bertha" two days before the weekend. Maybe we could make it a two-car convoy with the Buick and the Tempo (and *Mr. Kayak*... and Mom and Bertha and the traveling cat named Stick Tail). Margy wouldn't be able to join me on the Fraser that weekend, since she needed to take care of some personal errands in Bellingham (part of our complicated, simple life), but maybe she could assist with a kayak pullout and a ride back to my solo launch site. Sure, this would require kayaking alone in the big yellow banana rather than using the little yellow mango, since the small kayak was in the States (another aspect of the complicated, simple life). But I've kayaked in the big vessel by myself before, and the extra storage would be nice for an overnight trip. Thus, on relatively short notice, I begin planning the details.

So less than a week after hearing about the death of my all-time hero, 72-year-old Neil Armstrong, I'm well into detailed plans for a major river trip. Life suddenly seems all too short, and the kayak trip even more important.

* * * * *

THE WEATHER BEGINS TO LOOK BETTER than the original forecast for the Labor Day weekend. I plan an early ferry departure from Saltery Bay, with Margy and her mom to follow later in the day. I'd like to arrive at my launch location by mid-afternoon, with enough time to organize my gear and get to my first riverside campsite before dark.

Arriving at Langdale. where my second ferry of the day departs, I use my time in the waiting area to reorganize my camping gear. I've planned this trip in considerable detail, but loading the Tempo was a last-minute event when the weather forecast finally (and somewhat unexpectedly) fell into my comfort zone.

In the ferry lineup, I walk around the car, opening doors and trunk, and moving items into several small backpacks. Behind me a young couple sits in their SUV, both clicking away on their mobile devices. At the moment, I'm totally convinced this kayak trip will be worth my time. After all, I too could be wasting my time on the Internet, as I often do, instead of preparing to challenge the real world.

Aboard the *Queen of Coquitlam*, I find a forward-facing seat next to the window. I watch two teenage girls two rows in front of me in aft-facing seats. These cute teenagers, either sisters or good friends, both wear sunglasses, shorts, and T-shirts, while clicking away on their handhelds. I don't see them look up at the passing scenery even once during the entire journey to Horseshoe Bay.

The world is changing, and it's not for the better. Will future generations have any interest in exploring the great rivers of the world? By then, such adventures in life might only be experienced by clicking on tiny screens.

I want to interrupt the two girls, and ask them to at least glance at the beauty of Howe Sound, right out their window. But I'm not so bold, and I leave them to their clicking.

From Horseshoe Bay, I drive my normal path on Route 1, but when I reach the turnoff for the Aldergrove border crossing, I just keep going. I pass Abbotsford and Chilliwack, continuing farther than I've ever driven on this road. Although I've flown this route in my Piper Arrow many times, there's a new beauty from the ground. Mountains rise up on both sides, marking the borders of the great valley, carved out by the mighty Fraser River.

I exit at the sign that reads "Harrison Hot Springs," and continue north to the last ramp before the Agassiz Bridge passes over the Fraser. As I wind down to Ferry Road, which parallels the river, there's a good feel here. It's a nice blend of riverside beauty with a feeling of comfort at leaving the car in an area not totally remote.

Less than a mile downstream from the bridge, I turn off in a wide, hard-packed dirt area that provides easy access to the river. The launch spot I've scoped out on the map is much better than expected. Except for a small RV camper parked off to the side, this place is empty. (When I return 3 days later to retrieve the Tempo, this area is packed with more than a hundred people, a mix of overnight RVs and day visitors frolicking in the holiday sun.)

This is my first close look at the Fraser today, and I'm pleased the flow is less than I found on the Skagit River this same time of year. The current seems slightly more than half what I experienced on the Skagit, and the Fraser is much wider, so I expect no problems with the journey from here downstream.

In the dirt parking area a hundred feet from the water, I prepare to offload *Mr. Kayak* for the first time by myself, although I did load it alone rather easily by easing it up onto the Tempo from the rear. With its caddy wheels strapped to the stern, I pulled the kayak forward and lifted the bow onto the trunk (stop and rest), and then to the rear rooftop rack (lift, stop and rest again). Finally, I gave the big vessel a strong ass-push from the stern (lift, stop, rest, and adjust the kayak's position), until it was centered on the roof racks. Done!

Now I'm confident my solo offload will go just as smoothly, although in reverse. I attach the caddy wheels to the stern, where they fly in midair. Then I push *Mr. Kayak* backwards until its weight shifts enough to carry it gently down to its wheels. Another rearward tug, and I gently lower the bow onto trunk, ready to be hoisted the remaining short distance to the ground. No problem!

Behind the car, I load the kayak, not paying close attention to streamlined packaging and careful loading. As the boat's sole occupant, I'll have plenty of onboard storage for my camping gear. Plus, I have extra room in the normally-occupied forward cockpit. Even with the extra space, I make certain most of my gear is as far forward as possible, to prevent the kayak from riding low in the stern, as it tends to do with one person and no cargo.

While I'm loading *Mr. Kayak* behind the car, a fisherman in a tin boat pulls up onto shore. I walk over to ask him about river conditions, where to expect rapids, and the conditions near the Harrison River

Launch site on the Fraser River at Ferry Road

confluence where major roiling and even whirlpools are sometimes reported.

"Nothing special from the Harrison River this time of year," he explains. "Water is really low, and has been changing daily. You shouldn't have any problems. Expect the fastest current on the other shore, so you might want to stay along this side until you get used to it."

Excellent advice, and mighty comforting.

With the kayak now fully loaded, but still 50 feet from the water, I wheel it down to the river. I struggle a bit with the wheels in the soft sand, but it's easily manageable. I'm not sure how I'll launch by myself in the somewhat swift water near shore, but I figure it will all work out.

I back the kayak into the shallow water, and set the bow down on the beach, so the kayak isn't floating yet – bow on the sand and the stern almost buoyant with the caddy wheels still attached.

I step into the river next to *Mr. Kayak* (cool, but not cold in my neoprene boots). Then I use the kayak's aft carry handle to lift the stern a few inches, awkwardly remove the caddy wheels, and gradually test the situation by lowering the vessel back into the water. When I let go, the rear of the kayak immediately drifts downstream and grounds itself in the gravel near shore, with the bow still on the beach. The kayak is safe to leave (temporarily) while I return the wheels to the Tempo.

Then it's an easy launch by angling the bow into the water and pushing off from the stern while simultaneously hopping into the rear cockpit, my paddle dangling from one hand. Of course, it's more of a plop than a hop, and it takes a few seconds to slide down into the seat, with my feet stretching forward for the rudder pedals.

The bow doesn't swing around immediately, so I'm drifting downstream near shore, ass-end first. But a little paddling puts me on course without a lot of fuss. There's no way to do a launch like this without getting wet, but the water is not cold, and my boots are comfortable. I'm on my way.

Once I'm established comfortably in the kayak, I pull out my camera and snap a photo of the downstream scene. There's not much daylight left, but enough to paddle for a while and get a feel for the

Established downstream after launch

kayak loaded under these conditions. *Mr. Kayak* floats well with most of the cargo in front and me riding in the rear. The vessel feels comparable to the way it rides with two people aboard.

With everything now settled down, I'm busy organizing things in the cockpit. I check the GPS to determine the drift speed (3 to 6 miles per hour on most parts of the Fraser during this trip), search for my sunglasses, and... Look out!

When I look up, a huge logjam encompasses the area directly in front of me! From my perspective, it's moving from left to right at a frightening speed. I immediately recall a similar scary incident solo on the Skagit River, afterwards realizing it wasn't the logjam that was moving – it was me. And this is exactly the same situation. Everything seems to be moving rapidly to the right as I drift towards the left edge of the mass of grounded trees, with jutting trunks tilted at various attention-getting angles.

I push the left rudder, and start to paddle as fast as I can. But there isn't adequate room between the kayak and shore to clear the logjam on this side, so I push the right rudder and dig in my paddle with maximum force. Paddle! Paddle! Paddle!

I clear the big jam on the right side by only a few feet. In the first few minutes of my journey, I've already screwed up by not paying attention to my surroundings. It's a good lesson, and one that I fortunately survive.

Overall, the river is a joy to paddle. Logjams are generally not extensive, and there's always plenty of room to maneuver around them (if you're paying attention). A variety of recreational boats maneuver up and own the river, mostly small tin boats and bigger welded aluminum craft of various sizes. A lot of the boats are similar in design to the Harbercraft model I admire. Some of these metal boats have outboard motors, but most are equipped with jet drives that allow them to maneuver in shallow water near shore and safely pull up onto the beaches.

After an hour of paddling (mostly just steering as I drift), I closely parallel a gravel beach, watching a line of fishermen spaced about twenty feet apart. I drift past a dozen of them, spaced perfectly between each other with their lines in the water. I bet they'd love to be fishing a bit farther out from shore where I am, which reminds me this might be a good place to try trolling.

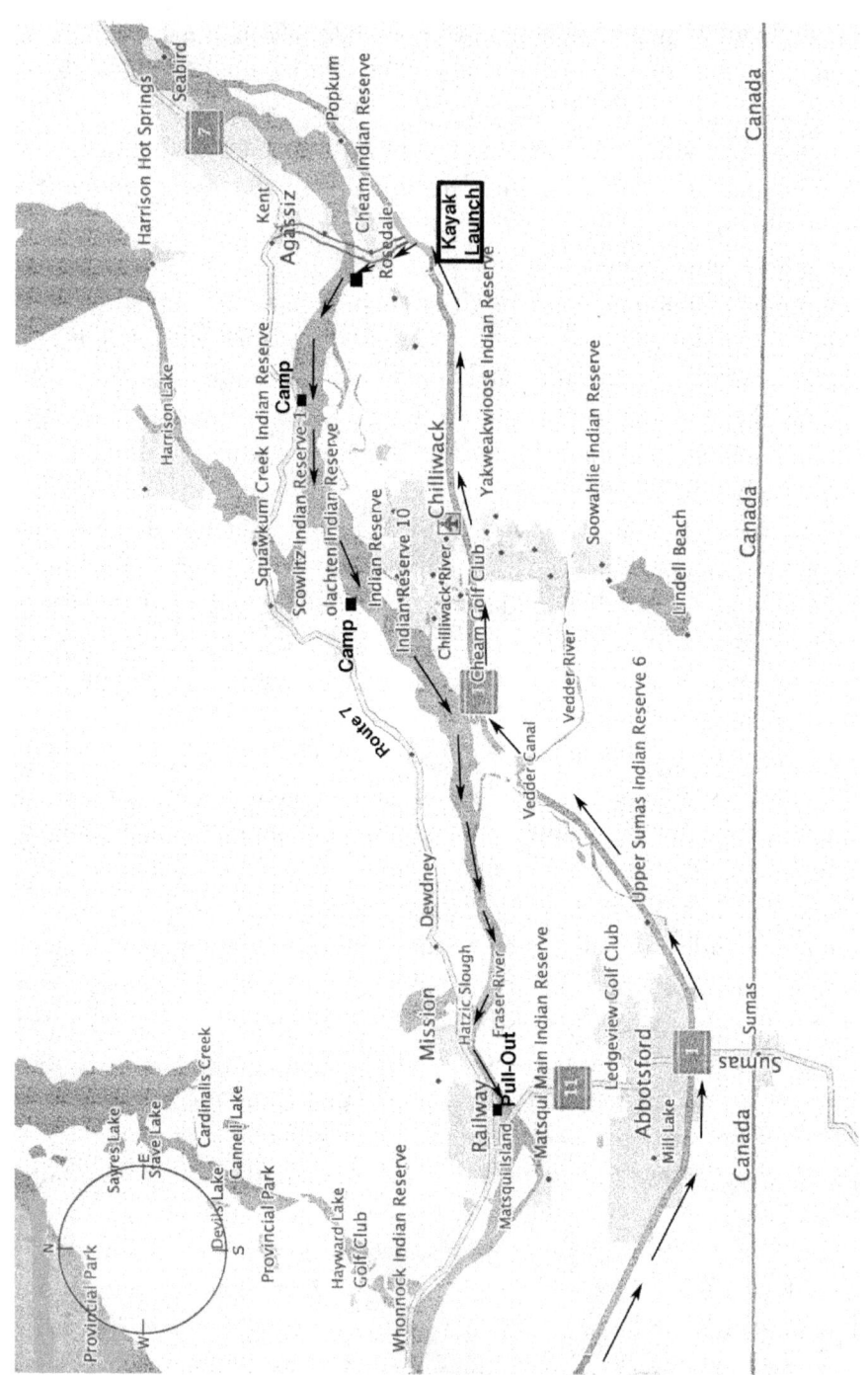

Fraser River, from Agassiz Bridge to Mission BC

I've brought along my fishing pole and a bright orange spinner, but I forgot to bring extra lures. Although I'm not sure about the depth of the water, I take my cue from those on shore. I throw out my line, and drag it behind me until the beach finally ends. Then I quickly retrieve my spinner before I lose it in my first hour on the river. With only one lure, I want to keep it safe and sound for trolling the next two days.

As I begin to look for a spot to spend the night, I find numerous potential sites that would work fine. The low water level has expanded the scope of the river's many islands, with numerous wide gravel beaches before reaching the line of bushes and trees. Meanwhile, I navigate around small logjams that are advertised in advance by the sound of rushing water pouring around them. How did I almost hit that first major jam?

In the distance, I hear a major cascade that sounds like a distant train. Then I hear the whistle, because it's a roaring freight train, traveling along the north shore. I wave, wondering if the whistle is for me.

Just before sunset, I select a wide gravel beach, and fight the current to get to shore. I misjudge the power of the flow, and I'm dragged downstream from where I'd like to land. Pointing the bow

Campsite on Fraser River

Moonrise on the Fraser River

back upstream, I struggle to overcome the current, but soon I'm in the less-intense flow near shore. I pull *Mr. Kayak* up onto the beach, and tie the bow to a nearby log that's lodged in the dirt.

After setting up my tent, I eat my snack meal, and watch the sky darken. It's not quite dark enough yet to see the first stars, but it should be a gorgeous night.

As I sit in my folding chair, a bright glow appears rather suddenly beyond a peak of the distant ridge, and I realize it's the almost-full moon rising in a majestic setting. When the moon finally pokes out from the edge of the mountain, I try a photo, but moonrise photos never come close to equaling the beauty of the event. Which is why we prefer some things without twenty-first century technology.

* * * * *

THE NEXT MORNING, I eat a light snack breakfast, and organize my gear for departure. I'm more organized today, splitting the load carried in the forward cockpit with the center hatch. I also move my spare twin-blade paddle to the hull area in front of me. When I launched from Ferry Road, the spare paddle was stowed (in its two segments) on the bow, which would have meant going swimming to get to it in an emergency.

With no wind, I make good progress at about 6 miles per hour while paddling sparingly. Often I elect to drift at 3 to 4 miles per hour, using the paddles only to assist the rudder in steering.

Numerous welded aluminum boats are out this morning, most of them trolling near the shore, with some boats tied to logjams where the occupants fish.

My original plan was to travel on the opposite side of the river in the area of the Harrison River outflow, to get a controlled feel of the famous current. But the river is too low to allow maneuvering near that shore, with small streams branching out where islands are shown on the map. Rather than risk getting grounded and possibly having to backtrack. I head right for the middle of the confluence of the two rivers, and it's little more than a minor roiling of the water.

Along the next island, I angle in close, trolling slow as I drift downstream. A Harbercraft-like aluminum boat trolls in the opposite direction near the shore. His outboard motor runs quiet, and we pass close, so I yell "Good Morning!"

"Trolling for alligators?" replies the fisherman in the bow.

"Alligators here?" I play along.

"Caught three so far today."

When I'm past the alligator fishermen, I give the fisherman's kidding remarks further thought. Maybe he was serious in his own frivolous way. Are there garfish here? They have beaklike jaws that might remind you of an alligator. No, I conclude, he was kidding about alligators, meaning tropical gators. An unusual sense of humor, maybe influenced by hours in the bow of a fishing boat.

I angle out into the middle of the big river, and let the kayak drift. This will be a good spot for lunch, which I carry in a waterproof bag in my cockpit. I drift, and eat, and drift some more.

In early afternoon I begin to look for a campsite. I have plenty of energy left to paddle farther, but my map shows the islands are ending, and they seem ideal for camping. So I stop early, planning to enjoy the afternoon on the beach in the sun.

Day #2 on the Fraser River

The spot I select is similar to the island site the previous night, another wide gravel beach left by the still-dropping water level at the end of summer. The early stop will leave me a reasonable paddle distance tomorrow, since I want to be at Mission in time for USC's first football game of the season. After checking the TV schedule, I reserved a motel room that will allow me to watch the game. Travel near and far, but never miss a USC game! (Most Pacific Northwest PAC-12 sports fans possess a similar passion for their teams, expressed as: Go Cougs! Go Dawgs! Go Ducks! Go Beavs!)

Coming to shore, I fight the current again, until it drops off near the beach. Finally ashore, I perform a walk-around inspection of the kayak. I don't normally perform such an examination, but the rudder clanked rather loudly as it fell into its storage position when I retracted it when coming to shore. Sure enough, the rudder retraction cord, previously frayed, is now broken. I carry a short spare cord for splicing, but it takes a full hour to complete the repair. (Even then, it's a temporary fix that will require a visit to a kayak shop soon.)

Island campsite, Day #2

Even with the unexpected repair time added on, my leisurely afternoon in the sun is wonderful. I do some reading, writing, and listen to the portable radio. But mostly I just sit by the shore and watch the water and the frequent passing of Labor Day boats. Can there be a better place to spend a holiday weekend than here? No reservations? No problem.

A red jet boat pulls onto shore about a half-mile upstream, and a family sets up their tent. Then a small tin boat pulls up next to them. A few minutes later, the man from the tin boat walks over to talk to me.

"Where did you launch?" he asks.

"Bellingham," I reply, throwing him a smile so this doesn't get out of hand.

"Eh?" he says, Canadian style, acting like he hasn't seen the flag on the stern of my beached kayak. "If you say so."

"Just kiddin'," I reply. Then I outline my route, and how I'll need to retrieve my car when I'm done.

The man explains that the river is extraordinarily low, making campsites on the gravel beaches more plentiful this time of year.

"What do you use for lures?" I ask, gesturing towards the family upstream, where three lines are in the water.

"Just a small ball of cotton and a marshmallow," he replies. "Mostly Chinook this late in the summer, but not many this year."

"I've been trolling as I drift," I say. "Using a bright orange spoon, but I'm not sure it's a good way to fish. The lure drags behind me, but it must be merely flowing with the current."

"Won't catch anything that way. Even with our marshmallows, it's more a matter of snagging them as they pass by than really catching them."

Still, I'm not convinced. My fluorescent lure is bright in the muddy water, and there must be salmon in these inviting waters. Plus, there are quite a few fishermen.

"It's no problem if I don't catch any fish," I offer. "I'm used to it."

The man gives me a final inquisitive look as he nods and walks away. He's found a fellow who says he launched his kayak in the States, and fishes with no apparent interest in catching anything. Probably an American.

That night, under another clear sky, the perfectly full moon rises over the mountain peaks, nearly an hour later than the previous night. Stars are out now, and big bonfires have popped up on the opposite shore, north of Chilliwack. Four fires are nearly directly across from my campsite. The biggest blaze is accompanied by celebratory yells that carry across almost a mile of water that separates us. Near that big fire, off-road vehicles throttle up and down, and headlights pop in and out of view. The bark of a dog carries across the river. Canadians are celebrating their holiday weekend.

* * * * *

THE NEXT DAY, I relax on shore until almost 11 o'clock. Today I expect at least 3 hours of paddling, but catching the beginning of the football game in the early evening shouldn't be a problem. When I finally launch and start downstream, aluminum boats pop up everywhere along the shore, most of them anchored, while their sterns and several fishing lines swing downstream. The wind picks up from the southwest, a nearly direct headwind, and waves accompany the wind.

Soon I'm in two-foot chop, and struggling to stay pointed downstream. Every time I take a break from paddling, the combination of wind, waves, and current tends to turn me around so my bow is backwards. For drifting, this is okay but not comfortable, since I'm concerned about logjams that may be too small to announce themselves by the rush of water. Plus, it's noisier now with such a strong wind (about 15 knots).

I troll while I drift, occasionally retrieving my lure to try a few casts to the sides. In one area, I watch a large salmon jump completely out of the water three times (or may 3 salmon leap only once). But my orange lure is untouched.

The waves increase until they're about 3 feet high, but *Mr. Kayak* handles them easily. After all, this is a sea kayak, very stable in waves, but the water splashes high enough to occasionally reach me in the back cockpit. On Powell Lake, 3-foot waves are my limit, but those

Rough water, Day #3

conditions include a longer wavelength, which seems worse than these tightly spaced sets.

Still, my forward progress is reduced by waves and wind that are moving upstream, and a constantly lessening current (about 2 mile per hour now) pushing downstream. The opposing forces of wind and current are obviously heightening the waves.

I pull over to the edge of the river, trying to find quieter water near shore. And it is quiet, but the current is even slower here, only 1 mile per hour. So I reach a compromise, paddling fairly near shore, at the edge of the big waves, all the way to Mission.

In one extensive stretch of nearly straight shoreline, a line of faded-red-and-white steel pilings mark the right side of the river, tie-up spots for log booms, with some of them harboring penned logs awaiting pickup. The pilings extent all the way to the next bend in the river (maybe beyond), and I count at least 30 of them, including a final row of wooden tripod pillars. The pilings seem perfectly spaced at about 200-foot intervals.

By this time, my paddling energy is dwindling, and I'm slowing even more. But the wind decreases as I exit the venturi effect of the tall mountains, and enter the much flatter lowland. The current has dropped to an average of only 2 miles per hour, even less in many spots. So I have some time on my hands, and I try a little mental math.

When I paddle, my blades hit the water on alternate sides, timed almost precisely at 60 strokes per minute. So every blade in the water equates to a second on my watch. Stroke, stroke, stroke – 40 seconds between pilings. That's about 200 feet (from my visual estimate) every 40 seconds, or 300 feet per minute. Which is 18,000 feet (300 X 60) per hour – about 3.5 miles per hour. I check my GPS, and it shows a reassuring 4.1 mph. The things you do with your mind when you have the time...

Three hours turn into four, but finally the bridge at Mission appears around the corner. On the right bank of the river sits the city's waterfront, an ugly looking line of pulp heaps and logging cranes. (I'll later find the town itself modern and interesting.) The marina is bigger than anticipated, but I expect it to be full on a holiday weekend. There should be enough room for a sea kayak somewhere.

Approaching Mission Bridge

I tie up under the outer gangway, where it looks like no one would moor permanently. The marina office is closed, but a sign provides an after-hours phone number. Bick, the harbor attendant, answers promptly. He sounds just like Jim, the wharfinger in Powell River who is one of my favorite people. Maybe all Canadian wharf managers are trained to sound the same.

"We can't leave you there, eh?" says Bick. "That outer finger gets blasted by the wakes of tugs and barges. It'll do your kayak no good."

Over the phone, Bick directs me to a more sheltered dock on an inner finger, perfect for *Mr. Kayak*. He asks me to drop "a five or ten dollar bill" in the mail slot at the office. It's the perfect overnight location for my kayak while I attend to the USC game. The next morning, Margy will drive up from Bellingham to shuttle me back to the Tempo near the Agassiz Bridge. Then I'll drive back to Mission, and pull Mr. Kayak out of the water at the marina's launch ramp, a complicated simple plan.

But today is not over yet. I walk from the marina to the motel, stopping for a hamburger along the way. After several days on the river

Mr. Kayak at Mission Marina BC

with relatively healthy snacks as meals, the tasty burger seems overly rich. And the French fries are either cooked in lard or seem that way after several days of avoiding the fast foods of a modern city. But I eat every last morsel.

I make it to the motel 10 minutes before kickoff. And USC wins the season opener, big-time. Between plays, I'm clicking around on the Internet.

Lazy river to booming city in three days. Once back in society, I'm quick to take advantage of its technology.

But I promise myself to look out the window every time I travel by ferry.

* * * * *

THE LESSON OF THIS RIVER TRIP is more universal than personal resolve to put away my electronic gadgets whenever I can. Whatever country, regardless of the size of the vessel, solo or otherwise, kayaking is a unique opportunity to escape from the pressures of society. There are plenty of recreational activities that promote freedom from our everyday responsibilities, but kayaking deserves a spot near the top of the list.

Once on the river (or lake or ocean), nature sweeps us away. More accurately, the surrounding environment allows us to sweep ourselves away. We take command of our kayak, and face the existing conditions. We maneuver from the launch site to a spot we decide is the appropriate place to end the journey. All that occurs on the water between point A and B is entirely up to us. Nowhere is free will more evident than when we execute the paddling decisions we make along the way. A paddle is a very powerful thing.

Stroke, stroke, stroke. One mile (or kilometer), and then another. And along the way, it's okay to occasionally stop paddling, and let the current take our kayak where it may.

About the Author

From 1980 to 2005, Wayne Lutz was Chairman of the Aeronautics Department at Mount San Antonio College in Los Angeles. He also served 20 years as a U.S. Air Force C-130 aircraft maintenance officer. His educational background includes a B.S. degree in physics from the University of Buffalo and an M.S. in systems management from the University of Southern California. The author is a flight instructor with 7000 hours of flying experience.

For three decades, he spent summers in Canada, exploring remote regions in his Piper Arrow and camping next to his airplane. The author resides in a floating cabin on Canada's Powell Lake in all seasons, and occasionally in a city-folk condo in Bellingham, Washington. His writing genres include regional Canadian publications and science fiction.

Books by Wayne J. Lutz

Coastal British Columbia Stories

Up the Lake
Up the Main
Up the Winter Trail
Up the Strait
Up the Airway
Farther Up the Lake
Farther Up the Main
Farther Up the Strait
Cabin Number 5
Off the Grid
Up the Inlet

Pacific Northwest Titles

Flying the Pacific Northwest
Paddling the Pacific Northwest

Science Fiction Titles

Echo of a Distant Planet
Inbound to Earth
Anomaly at Fortune Lake
When Galaxies Collide
Across the Galactic Sea

Order at: www.PowellRiverBooks.com

Appendix
Geographic Index

Abbotsford BC   p.155
Acme WA   p.92-96
Agassiz BC   p.155, 160
Albany OR   p.138-139, 144, 147, 149-152
Aldergrove BC   p.16, 155
Bellingham WA   p.13, 17, 19-20, 25-27, 125, 131, 138
Birdsview WA   p.29, 33-34, 36
Blaine WA   p.115, 117, 121
Bower Roack State Park OR   p.149-150
Burlington WA   p. 13, 21, 69-70, 77, 79, 86, 102
California Creek WA   p.118, 131-137
Chilliwack BC   p.155, 166
Columbia River OR   p.138
Concrete WA   p.25, 28, 31-32, 50, 65
Conway WA   p.58, 62-63, 65, 67
Corvallis OR   p.138-148, 152
Dakota Creek WA   p.115-124, 131
Deming WA   p.72
Dodd Narrows BC   p.12
Drayton Harbor WA   p.117-121, 132, 134
Euguene OR   p.138
Fir Island WA   p.65-66
Fraser River BC   p.10, 14, 153-170
Hamilton WA   p.45-47, 71, 102, 104, 106
Harrison Hot Springs BC p.155
Harrison River BC   p.156-157, 163
Horseshoe Bay BC   p.16, 155
Horseshoe Lake BC   p.91
Lake Samish WA   p.125-130
Lang Bay BC   p.11

Langdale BC p.155
Lois Lake BC p.88
Lyman WA p.47-51, 56, 102, 106
Maple Falls WA p.109
Marblemont WA p.31
Milltown WA p.67
Mission BC p.160, 164, 168-170
Mount Vernon WA p.21
Nanton Lake BC p.91
Nooksack River WA p.13, 68, 71-75, 92-101, 109
Norway Island (Gulf Islands) BC p.89
Portland OR p.138
Powell Lake BC p.10-11, 16, 68-70, 87, 89-90
Powell River BC p.10, 12, 16, 68
Rasar State Park WA p.23, 25, 29-31, 36-42, 44, 46
Rockport WA p.31, p52
Ross Island (Skagit River) WA p.40, 46, 53-59, 62
Salem OR p.138
Saltery Bay BC p.154
Sedro-Wooley WA p.28-29, 60-61, 77, 80-82
Silver Lake WA p.109-114
Skagit River WA p.13, 20-21, 25, 28, 31-33, 36, 44, 46, 53, 62-67, 69, 77, 79, 81, 85, 102-108, 115
Skagit Wildlife Recreation Area WA p.65
Stillaguamish River p.126
Telegraph Harbour (Gulf Island) BC p.88
Van Zandt WA p.92, 96
Willamette River p.138-152

Coastal British Columbia Stories
A Regional Series of Books by Wayne J. Lutz

Order at:
www.PowellRiverBooks.com

Coastal BC Living Blog
PowellRiverBooks.blogspot.com

www.ingramcontent.com/pod-product-compliance
Lightning Source LLC
Chambersburg PA
CBHW071733080526
44588CB00013B/2016